Free Video  **Free Video**

Essential Test Tips Video from Trivium Test Prep

Dear Customer,

Thank you for purchasing from Trivium Test Prep! We're honored to help you prepare for your GED exam.

To show our appreciation, we're offering a **FREE** *GED Essential Test Tips* **Video by Trivium Test Prep.*** Our video includes 35 test preparation strategies that will make you successful on the GED. All we ask is that you email us your feedback and describe your experience with our product. Amazing, awful, or just so-so: we want to hear what you have to say!

To receive your **FREE** *GED Essential Test Tips* **Video**, please email us at 5star@ triviumtestprep.com. Include "Free 5 Star" in the subject line and the following information in your email:

1. The title of the product you purchased.

2. Your rating from 1 – 5 (with 5 being the best).

3. Your feedback about the product, including how our materials helped you meet your goals and ways in which we can improve our products.

4. Your full name and shipping address so we can send your **FREE** *GED Essential Test Tips* **Video**.

If you have any questions or concerns please feel free to contact us directly at 5star@ triviumtestprep.com.

Thank you!

– Trivium Test Prep Team

*To get access to the free video please email us at 5star@triviumtestprep.com, and please follow the instructions above.

GED Reasoning Through Language Arts Study Guide

Comprehensive Review with Practice Test Questions for the GED Exam

Table of Contents

Introduction

Congratulations on choosing to take the GED exam! By purchasing this book, you've taken an important step on your path to earning your high school-equivalency credential.

This guide will provide you with a detailed overview of the GED exam so that you know exactly what to expect on test day. We'll take you through all the concepts covered on the exam and give you the opportunity to test your knowledge with practice questions. Even if it's been a while since you last took a major test, don't worry; we'll make sure you're more than ready!

What is the GED?

The General Educational Development, or GED, test is a high school-equivalency test—composed of four subtests—that certifies that the test-taker has high school-level academic skills. Forty states currently offer the GED test. The four subtests can be taken together or separately, but you must pass all four subtests in order to pass the test overall. Once a test-taker in one of those states passes the exam, then that person becomes eligible to receive a high school-equivalency diploma, which can be used in job applications or in applying to colleges or universities. The test is specifically designed for individuals who did not complete a high school diploma, no matter the reason.

What's on the GED?

The GED test gauges high school-level content knowledge and skills in four areas: Reasoning through Language Arts (RLA), Mathematical Reasoning, Science, and Social Studies. Candidates are expected to be able to read closely, write clearly, edit and understand standard written English as it is used in context, and solve quantitative and algebraic problems. You also must show strong content knowledge in life science, physical science, and Earth and space science as well as civics and government, United States history, geography and the world, and economics.

The test includes a variety of question types, including multiple-choice, drag-and-drop, hot spot, and fill-in-the-blank. The multiple-choice questions are a standard style in which the test-taker selects the best answer among a series of choices. In drag-and-drop questions, the test-taker must select the best answer, click on it, and drag it to the appropriate location. This usually involves sorting items into categories or making associations between different concepts. Hot spot questions require the test-taker to click on a specific area of an image. For fill-in-the-blank questions, the test-taker must type in the word or phrase missing from the statement or question. The Reasoning through Language Arts section also includes some questions in which the test-taker must select the best grammatical or punctuation change from a drop-down list of options as well as extended response questions that require the test-taker to type the answer.

Each subtest is taken separately. You must complete one subtest before moving on to the next. You will have 115 minutes for the math test, ninety minutes for the science test, seventy minutes for the social studies test, and 150 minutes for the Reasoning through Language Arts test.

What's on the GED Exam?		
SKILLS ASSESSED	TOPICS	PERCENTAGE OF EXAM*
Reasoning Through Language Arts		
▶ Read closely	Informational texts	75%
▶ Write clearly		
▶ Edit and understand the use of standard written English in context	Literature texts	25%
Mathematical Reasoning		
▶ Understand key mathematical concepts	Quantitative problem-solving	45%
▶ Demonstrate skill and fluency with key math procedures	Algebraic problem-solving	55%
▶ Apply concepts to realistic situations		
Science		
▶ Use scientific reasoning (textually and quantitatively)	Life science	40%
	Physical science	40%
▶ Apply scientific reasoning to a variety of realistic situations	Earth and space science	20%

SKILLS ASSESSED	TOPICS	PERCENTAGE OF EXAM*
Social Studies		
▶ Textual analysis ▶ Data representation ▶ Inference skills ▶ Problem-solving using social studies content	Civics and government	50%
	United States history	20%
	Economics	15%
	Geography and the world	15%

Percentages are approximate.

The Reasoning through Language Arts test assesses your ability to understand a range of texts which can be found in both academic and workplace settings. The test includes literary and informational texts as well as important US founding documents. The texts vary in length from 450 to 900 words. You will be asked to identify details and make logical inferences from—as well as valid claims about—the texts. You also will be asked to define key vocabulary and use textual evidence to analyze the texts in your own words in the form of a written response.

The Mathematical Reasoning test assesses mastery of key fundamental math concepts. Rather than focusing on specific content, the test focuses on reasoning skills and modes of thinking that can be used in a variety of mathematical content areas, specifically algebra, data analysis, and number sense. Questions will assess your ability to make sense of complex problems, use logical thinking to find solutions, recognize structure, and look for and express regularity in repeated reasoning. You also will be evaluated on the precision of your mathematics.

The Science test assesses your mastery of scientific content in life science, physical science, and Earth and space science, as well as your ability to apply scientific reasoning. Each question on the test will focus on one science practice and one content topic. Specifically, questions will relate to two primary themes: Human Health and Living Systems—all concepts related to the health and safety of all living things on the planet—and Energy and Related Systems—all concepts related to sources and uses of energy.

The Social Studies test assesses your mastery of both social studies content and skills. Each question addresses one element of social studies practice and one specific content topic. The primary focus of the test is on American civics and government, with the other three content areas as supplements. The questions address two core themes: Development of Modern Liberties and Democracy—which traces the current ideas of democracy from ancient times to present—and Dynamic Responses in Societal Systems, which addresses how society's systems, structures, and policies have developed and responded to each other.

Unique Question Types

While the majority of the GED exam is made up of multiple-choice questions, it also contains several other types of questions that might be unfamiliar to you. Collectively, these are called "technology-enhanced items" because they require you to interact with a computer. There are four types of these questions: drag-and-drop, hot spot, drop-down or cloze, and fill-in-the-blank. Each type of question is structured a little differently and requires different actions from the test-taker. Each type of question also assesses different skills. While they may seem a little intimidating, once you understand what these questions are testing and how to answer them, you will see they are quite manageable.

DRAG-and-DROP

A drag-and-drop question has three parts: the question or prompt, drop target, and tiles or "draggers." Each tile contains a small image, word, or numerical expression. You will read the question or prompt, and then click the tile you think has the correct answer, drag it to the target area, and then let it go. In some cases, you may be able to put more than one tile in a single target area, or you may be able to put the same tile in multiple target areas. If this is the case, a note included with the question will tell you that. For example, imagine a question says, *Classify the following fruits by color.* There is a response area for yellow, blue, green, and red, and tiles that say *apple, strawberry, blueberry, banana,* and *pear.* You would drag both the apple and strawberry tiles to the red target area. You would also put the apple tile in the green area.

Drag-and-drop questions will differ both in structure and in skills assessed, depending on the subtest. On the Mathematics subtest, drag-and-drop questions are primarily used for constructing expressions, equations, and inequalities. For example, the prompt will include a scenario and an incomplete equation. The tiles will contain various numerical and/or alphabetical variables and operators that could complete the equation. You must then drag the appropriate mathematical element to its spot in the equation. You also could be asked to order the steps in a mathematical process or solution or match items from two different sets.

On the Reasoning Through Language Arts (RLA) subtest, drag-and-drop questions will typically focus on sequencing and classifying to assess comprehension and analysis of a reading passage. Some questions may ask you to order events in a passage based on chronology or to illustrate cause and effect. Or you might be asked to classify evidence based on how it relates to the argument of a passage. Drag-and-drop questions on this subtest will usually incorporate graphic organizers, such as Venn diagrams, timelines, or charts.

On the Social Studies subtest, drag-and-drop questions are primarily used for mapping, classifying, and sequencing. For example, you might be asked to put the steps in a political process in the correct order, or you may be asked to sort actions based on the related constitutional freedom. Alternatively, you could be asked to place correct labels on the continents or use information from a brief text to place data points on a graph or chart.

On the Science subtest, drop-and-drag questions are used primarily for sequencing questions: placing the steps of a biological or chemical process in the correct order. These questions can also be used for classification, like sorting animals into mammals and non-mammals. Like on the RLA subtest, science drag-and-drop questions often utilize graphic organizers, like Venn diagrams.

EXAMPLE

1. The owner of a taco truck decides to use data to determine how many tacos he can make during a two-hour lunch rush. He has determined that the average time it takes to make five tacos is eight minutes.

   Complete the equation to show how the taco truck owner determined that he can make seventy-five tacos in two hours.

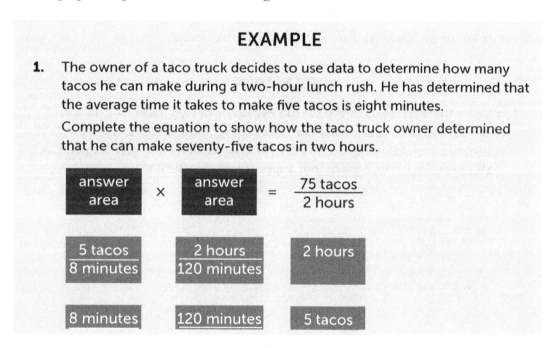

HOT SPOT

In a hot spot question, you will be presented with a graphic image. The image is embedded with virtual "sensors" placed at various points. The question will ask you to identify something specific within the image or to select an answer from several listed within the image. You will indicate your selection by clicking on a virtual sensor. For example, the image could be a diagram of the human body. If the question asks where the lungs are located, you would click the chest, activating the sensor there. While hot spot questions are different from a traditional multiple-choice question, they might be easier for you to do. Clicking on part of an image—rather than selecting a choice from A to D—might feel similar to how you express knowledge in the real world.

Hot spot questions appear on every subtest except RLA. On the Mathematics subtest, hot spots are most often used to assess your ability to plot points on coordinate grids, number lines, or scatter plots. For example, the graphic image could be a coordinate grid, and the question would ask you to plot a specific point, like (5, –2). You would then click the spot on the graph associated with (5, –2). Other math questions include identifying specific parts of a scale model, selecting numerical or algebraic expressions that identify parallel equations, or identifying different representations of the same numeric value.

On the Science subtest, hot spot questions may use a graphic image or a block of text. In addition to allowing you to identify information on a model or diagram, they assess your understanding of the relationship between data points or your ability to use data points to support or refute a particular conclusion.

On the Social Studies subtest, hot spots questions often ask you to indicate evidence that supports a particular statement or idea. Like on the Science subtest, you might be asked to demonstrate the relationship between different data points from a short block of text or an image. They are also often used with mapping.

EXAMPLE

2. The square below is based on the eye color of two parents: one with brown eyes and one with green. According to this square, this couple's biological children have a 50 percent chance of having green eyes. Click the sections of the square that support this conclusion.

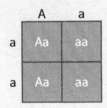

DROP-DOWN (CLOZE)

A drop-down question is an open-stem question, or incomplete statement. This type of question occurs in multiple-choice questions as well. However, in a drop-down question, rather than selecting an answer from the A – D options that appear after the statement, a drop-down box with multiple response options is embedded in the statement. You will select the appropriate word or phrase, which will fill in the blank. You can then read the complete statement to check the accuracy of your response. For example, a question might read, *Bananas are*, followed by a drop-down box with several colors listed—blue, red, yellow, green. You would click yellow, and the statement would then read, *Bananas are yellow*.

On the Mathematics subtest, drop-down questions are most often used to assess math vocabulary or to compare two quantities, in which case the drop-down box will contain less than, greater than, and equal signs. For other drop-down questions, you will be asked to select the correct number to complete a statement.

On the RLA subtest, drop-down questions are used to assess mastery of language skills, such as American English conventions, standard usage, and punctuation. Drop-down questions on this subtest mimic the editing process. So multiple variations of the same phrase will appear in the drop-down box within the text, and you will select the one that is grammatically correct. It is important to read the complete sentence after your selection to ensure your choice makes sense.

On the Science and Social Studies subtests, these questions are also most often used with text. You may be asked to draw a logical conclusion from provided text-based evidence or to make a generalization based on an author's argument.

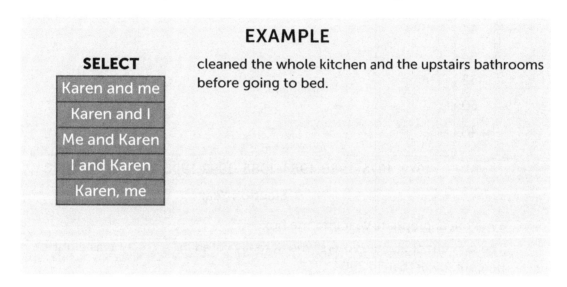

FILL-IN-THE-BLANK (FIB)

A fill-in-the-blank (FIB) question is a combination of a standard item and a constructed response. It is similar to a drop-down question in that it contains an incomplete statement. However, rather than selecting an answer from several options, you type in the answer. Unlike a constructed response, the answer you type will be only one to two words long. Using the example in the drop-down section, if the statement read, *Bananas are*, rather than selecting from several colors, you would simply type *yellow*. FIB can only be used for questions in which the answers have very little variability (so this particular example would not actually appear on the test). Sometimes a question may have more than one blank, requiring you to type two separate responses. FIB questions assess your knowledge without the distraction of incorrect choices.

FIB questions are included in all subtests except the RLA subtest. On the Mathematics subtest, FIB questions may ask you to type a numerical answer to a math problem or to write an equation using the numbers and characters on the keyboard. On the Science subtest, an FIB question may ask you to fill in the specific quantity of something from a graphic representation of data or for a response to a specific calculation.

On the Social Studies subtest, FIB questions are used to assess your understanding of a concept or key vocabulary. Often there will be brief text from which you will have to infer the concept or vocabulary. Other questions will ask you to identify specific information—from a chart, graph, or map—that supports or demonstrates a concept, idea, or trend.

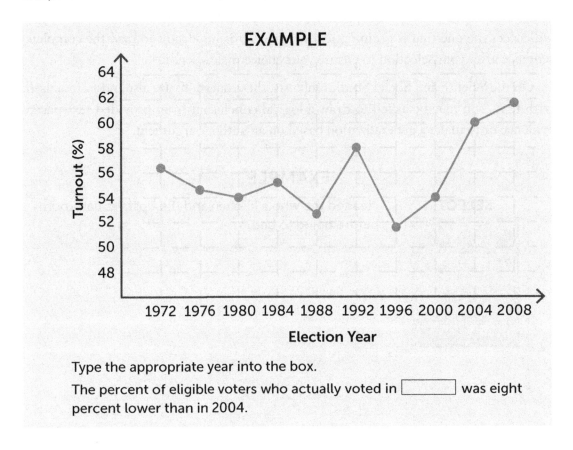

EXAMPLE

Type the appropriate year into the box.

The percent of eligible voters who actually voted in ☐ was eight percent lower than in 2004.

How is the GED Scored?

You will receive your scores on your GED tests within twenty-four hours of completing the exam.

The number of raw points each question is worth depends on the number of required answers for that question. For example, a question that requires the test-taker to select two items from a drop-down menu would be worth two raw points.

The two science constructed-response questions are scored on a three-point scale. Scores are based on scientific reasoning, the application of relevant scientific skills, and the quality of the evidence or support provided.

The written component of the Reasoning through Language Arts subtest is scored on three traits: analysis of arguments and use of evidence, development of ideas and structure, and clarity and command of standard English. Each trait can earn a raw score of up to two points.

The number of questions can vary between versions of the exam but the number of raw points remains constant. There are sixty-five raw score points on the Reasoning through Language Arts exam, forty-nine on the Mathematical Reasoning exam, forty on the Science exam, and thirty on the Social Studies exam. The total number of raw points earned is then scaled to a score between 100 and 200. You must earn at least 145 scaled score points in order to qualify for your high school equivalency credential. A score of at least 165 qualifies you as College Ready, and a score of 175 or higher qualifies you as College Ready + Credit, meaning you could qualify to receive college credit.

Each test is scored independently, and points from one test cannot affect the point value of another. You must pass each subtest in order to qualify for your high school-equivalency credential.

There is no guessing penalty on the GED exam, so you should always guess if you do not know the answer to a question.

How is the GED Administered?

The GED exam is a computer-based test offered at a wide range of sites throughout the United States and the world. To find a test center near you, check with Pearson VUE.

You will need to print your registration ticket from your online account and bring it, along with your identification, to the testing site on test day. Some test centers will require other forms or documentation, so make sure to check with your test center in advance. No pens, pencils, erasers, printed or written materials, electronic devices or calculators are allowed. An online scientific calculator will be provided to you at the time of the test as well as a formula reference sheet for the math test. Check in advance with your testing center for specific testing guidelines, including restrictions on dress and accessories.

You may take the subtests all on the same day or individually on separate days. There is no required order for completing the test. Certain jurisdictions may apply limits to the amount of time available for completing all four tests.

There are three versions of each test, so if you want to retake the test, you can do so right away up to two times. You will receive a different version of the test each time. If you still need to retake the test after the third time, you must wait sixty days. Ultimately, you may take each test up to eight times a year. If you do not pass one subtest, you are not required to retake all of the tests—only the one you failed.

About This Guide

This guide will help you to master the most important test topics and also develop critical test-taking skills. We have built features into our books to prepare you for your tests and increase your score. Along with a detailed summary of the test's format, content, and scoring, we offer an in-depth overview of the content knowledge required to pass the test. In the review you'll find sidebars that provide interesting information, highlight key concepts, and review content so that you can solidify your understanding of the exam's concepts. You can also test your knowledge with sample questions throughout the text and practice questions that reflect the content and format of the GED. We're pleased you've chosen Accepted, Inc. to be a part of your journey!

CHAPTER ONE
Reading

To do well on reading comprehension questions on the GED, you should be able to identify explicit details in a text, draw inferences about the text, grasp the author's intent, and understand the main idea of a text. Just like the rest of the Reasoning Through Language Arts section, about 75 percent of the texts are from informational sources and 25 percent are literary.

The Main Idea

The main idea of a text describes the author's main topic and general concept; it also generalizes the author's point of view about a subject. It is contained within and throughout the text. The reader can find the main idea by considering how the main topic is addressed throughout a passage. On reading questions, you are expected not only to identify the main idea but also to be able to differentiate it from a text's theme and to summarize the main idea clearly and concisely. For instance, you might be asked to pick an answer choice that best summarizes the main idea of a passage.

The main idea is closely connected to topic sentences and how they are supported in a text. Questions may deal with finding topic sentences, summarizing a text's ideas, or locating supporting details. The sections and practice examples that follow detail the distinctions between these aspects of text.

DID YOU KNOW?
The author's perspective on the subject of the text and how he or she has framed the argument or story hints at the main idea. For example, if the author framed the story with a description, image, or short anecdote, he or she is hinting at a particular idea or point of view.

IDENTIFYING the MAIN IDEA

To identify the main idea, first identify the topic. The difference between these two things is simple: the **TOPIC** is the overall subject matter of a passage; the **MAIN IDEA** is what the author wants to say about that topic. The main idea covers the author's direct perspective about a topic, as distinct from the **THEME**, which is a generally true idea that the reader might derive from a text. Most of the time, fiction has a theme, whereas non-fiction has a main idea. This is the case because in a nonfiction text, the author speaks more directly to the audience about a topic—his or her perspective is more visible. For example, the following passage conveys the topic as well as what the author wants to communicate about that topic.

> The "shark mania" of recent years can be largely pinned on the sensationalistic media surrounding the animals: from the release of *Jaws* in 1975 to the week of ultra-hyped shark feeding frenzies and "worst shark attacks" countdowns known as *Shark Week*, popular culture both demonizes and fetishizes sharks until the public cannot get enough. Swimmers and beachgoers may look nervously for the telltale fin skimming the surface, but the reality is that shark bites are extremely rare and they are almost never unprovoked. Sharks attack people at very predictable times and for very predictable reasons. Rough surf, poor visibility, or a swimmer sending visual and physical signals that mimic a shark's normal prey are just a few examples.
>
> Of course, some places are just more dangerous to swim. Shark attack "hot spots," such as the coasts of Florida, South Africa, and New Zealand try a variety of solutions to protect tourists and surfers. Some beaches employ "shark nets," meant to keep sharks away from the beach, though these are controversial because they frequently trap other forms of marine life as well. Other beaches use spotters in helicopters and boats to alert beach officials when there are sharks in the area. In addition, there is an array of products that claim to offer personal protection from sharks, ranging from wetsuits in different colors to devices that broadcast electrical signals in an attempt to confuse the sharks' sensory organs. At the end of the day, though, beaches like these remain dangerous, and swimmers must assume the risk every time they paddle out from shore.

The author of this passage has a clear topic: sharks and their relationship with humans. In order to identify the main idea of the passage, the reader must ask, What does the author want to say about this topic? What is the reader meant to think or understand?

DID YOU KNOW?

Readers should identify the topic of a text and pay attention to how the details about it relate to one another. A passage may discuss, for example, topic similarities, characteristics, causes, and/ or effects.

The author makes sure to provide information about several different aspects of the relationship between sharks and humans, and points out that humans must respect sharks as dangerous marine animals, without sensationalizing the risk of attack. The reader can figure this out by looking at the various pieces of information the author includes as well as the similarities between them. The passage describes sensationalistic media, then talks about how officials and governments try to protect beaches, and ends with the observation that people must take personal responsibility. These details clarify what the author's main idea is: thanks to safety precautions and their natural behavior, sharks are not as dangerous as they are portrayed to be. Summarizing that main idea by focusing on the connection between the different details helps the reader draw a conclusion.

EXAMPLES

The art of the twentieth and twenty-first centuries demonstrates several aspects of modern social advancement. A primary example is the advent of technology: new technologies have developed new avenues for art making, and the globalization brought about by the internet has both diversified the art world and brought it together simultaneously. Even as artists are able to engage in a global conversation about the categories and characteristics of art, creating a more uniform understanding, they can now express themselves in a diversity of ways for a diversity of audiences. The result has been a rapid change in how art is made and consumed.

1. This passage is primarily concerned with
  A) the importance of art in the twenty-first century.
  B) the use of art to communicate overarching ideals to diverse communities.
  C) the importance of technology to art criticism.
  D) the change in understanding and creation of art in the modern period.

2. Which of the following best describes the main idea of the passage?
  A) Modern advances in technology have diversified art making and connected artists to distant places and ideas.
  B) Diversity in modern art is making it harder for art viewers to understand and talk about that art.
  C) The use of technology to discuss art allows us to create standards for what art should be.
  D) Art-making before the invention of technology such as the internet was disorganized and poorly understood.

TOPIC and SUMMARY SENTENCES

Identifying the main idea requires understanding the structure of a piece of writing. In a short passage of one or two paragraphs, the topic and summary sentences quickly relate what the paragraphs are about and what conclusions the author wants the reader to draw. These sentences function as bookends to a paragraph or passage, telling readers what to think and keeping the passage tied tightly together.

Generally, the TOPIC SENTENCE is the first, or very near the first, sentence in a paragraph. It is a general statement that introduces the topic, clearly and specifically directing the reader to access any previous experience with that topic.

The SUMMARY SENTENCE, on the other hand, frequently—but not always!—comes at the end of a paragraph or passage, because it wraps up all the ideas presented. This sentence provides an understanding of what the author wants to say about the topic and what conclusions to draw about it. While a topic sentence acts as an introduction to a topic, allowing the reader to activate his or her own ideas and experiences, the summary statement asks the reader to accept the author's ideas about that topic. Because of this, a summary sentence helps the reader quickly identify a piece's main idea.

EXAMPLES

There is nowhere more beautiful and interesting than California. With glimmering azure seas, fertile green plains, endless deserts, and majestic mountains, California offers every landscape. Hikers can explore the wilderness in Yosemite National Park, where a variety of plants and animals make their home. Farmers grow almonds, apricots, cotton, tomatoes, and more in the Central Valley that winds through the middle of the state. Skiers enjoy the slopes and backcountry of the Sierra Nevada and Lake Tahoe area. In the desert of Death Valley, temperatures rise well over one hundred degrees Fahrenheit. And of course, California's famous beaches stretch from the Mexican border to Oregon. Furthermore, California features some of America's most important cities. In the south, Los Angeles is home to the movie industry and Hollywood. Farther north, the San Francisco Bay Area includes Silicon Valley, where the US tech industry is based. Both places are centers of commercial activity. In fact, California is the most populous state in the country. There is no shortage of things to do or sights to see!

3. Which of the following best explains the general idea and focus indicated by the topic sentence?
   A) The diversity of California's landscape allows agriculture to flourish, and the most important crops will be detailed.
   B) California is beautiful and diverse; the reader will read on to find out what makes it so interesting.
   C) California is a peaceful place; its people live with a sense of predictability and the state is prosperous.
   D) The incredible geography of California is the reason it is a rural state, and the reader can expect a discussion of the countryside.

4. Which of the following best states what the author wants the reader to understand after reading the summary sentence?
   A) Tourists should see everything in California when they visit.
   B) The cities of California are interesting, but the rural parts are better.
   C) The resources of California are nearly exhausted.
   D) California is an inspiring and exciting place.

Supporting Details

Between a topic sentence and a summary sentence, the rest of a paragraph is built with **SUPPORTING DETAILS**. Supporting details come in many forms; the purpose of the passage dictates the type of details that will support the main idea. A persuasive passage may use facts and data or detail specific reasons for the author's opinion. An informative passage will primarily use facts about the topic to support the main idea. Even a narrative passage will have supporting details—specific things the author says to develop the story and characters.

The most important aspect of supporting details is exactly what it sounds like: they support the main idea. Examining the various supporting details and how they work with one another will reveal how the author views a topic and what the main idea of the passage is. Supporting details are key to understanding a passage.

Supporting details can often be found in texts by looking for **SIGNAL WORDS**—transitions that explain to the reader how one sentence or idea is connected to another. Signal words can add information, provide counterarguments, create organization in a passage, or draw conclusions. Some common signal words and phrases include *in particular, in addition, besides, contrastingly, therefore,* and *because.*

EXAMPLE

Increasingly, companies are turning to subcontracting services rather than hiring full-time employees. This provides companies with advantages like greater flexibility, reduced legal responsibility to employees, and lower possibility of unionization within the company. However, this has led to increasing confusion and uncertainty over the legal definition of employment. Courts have grappled with questions about the hiring company's responsibility in maintaining fair labor practices. Companies argue that they delegate that authority to subcontractors, while unions and other worker advocate groups argue that companies still have a legal obligation to the workers who contribute to their business.

5. According to the passage, why do companies use subcontractors?

Hiring subcontractors

   A) costs less money than hiring full-time employees.

   B) increases the need for unionization of employees.

   C) reduces the company's legal responsibilities.

   D) gives the company greater control over worker's hours.

The Author's Purpose

The author of a passage sets out with a specific goal in mind: to communicate a particular idea to an audience. The AUTHOR'S PURPOSE is determined by asking why the author wants the reader to understand the passage's main idea. There are four basic purposes to which an author can write: narrative, expository, technical, and persuasive. Within each of these general purposes, the author may direct the audience to take a clear action or respond in a certain way.

The purpose for which an author writes a passage is also connected to the structure of that text. In a NARRATIVE, the author seeks to tell a story, often to illustrate a theme or idea the reader needs to consider. In a narrative, the author uses characteristics of storytelling, such as chronological order, characters, and a defined setting, and these characteristics communicate the author's theme or main idea.

In an EXPOSITORY passage, on the other hand, the author simply seeks to explain an idea or topic to the reader. The main idea will probably be a factual statement or a direct assertion of a broadly held opinion. Expository writing can come in many forms, but one essential feature is a fair and balanced representation of a topic. The author may explore one detailed aspect or a broad range of characteristics, but he or she mainly seeks to prompt a decision from the reader.

Similarly, in TECHNICAL writing, the author's purpose is to explain specific processes, techniques, or equipment in order for the reader to use that process or equipment to obtain a desired result. Writing like this employs chronological or spatial structures, specialized vocabulary, and imperative or directive language.

DID YOU KNOW?
Reading persuasive text requires an awareness of what the author believes about the topic.

In PERSUASIVE writing, the author actively seeks to convince the reader to accept an opinion or belief. Much like expository writing, persuasive writing is presented in many organizational forms.

EXAMPLE

University of California, Berkeley, researchers decided to tackle an age-old problem: why shoelaces come untied. They recorded the shoelaces of a volunteer walking on a treadmill by attaching devices to record the acceleration, or g-force, experienced by the knot. The results were surprising. A shoelace knot experiences more g-force from a person walking than any rollercoaster can generate. However, if the person simply stomped or swung their feet—the two movements that make up a walker's stride—the g-force was not enough to undo the knots.

6. What is the purpose of this passage?
   A) to confirm if shoelaces always come undone
   B) to compare the force of treadmills and rollercoasters
   C) to persuade readers to tie their shoes tighter
   D) to describe the results of an experiment on shoelaces

Organization and Text Structures

It's important to analyze the organization and structure of informational texts, as these details can provide valuable insight into the author's purpose and the overall meaning of a text. Several common structures are used in informative texts, and understanding these structures will help readers quickly make sense of new texts. Texts may be organized in one of the following ways:

▶ CHRONOLOGICAL texts describe events in the order they occurred.

▶ PROBLEM-SOLUTION texts begin by describing a problem and then offer a possible solution to the issue.

▶ CAUSE-EFFECT is a text structure that shows a causal chain of events or ideas.

▶ GENERAL-TO-SPECIFIC is a text structure that describes a general topic then provides details about a specific aspect of that topic.

▶ COMPARE-CONTRAST texts give the similarities and differences between two things.

Authors choose the organizational structure of their text according to their purpose. For example, an author who hopes to convince people to begin recycling might begin by talking about the problems that are caused by excessive waste and end by offering recycling as a reasonable solution. On the other hand, the author might choose to use a chronological structure for an article whose purpose is to give an impartial history of recycling.

EXAMPLE

For thirteen years, a spacecraft called *Cassini* was on an exploratory mission to Saturn. The spacecraft was designed not to return but to end its journey by diving into Saturn's atmosphere. This dramatic ending provided scientists with unprecedented information about Saturn's atmosphere and its magnetic and gravitational fields. First, however, *Cassini* passed Saturn's largest moon, Titan, where it recorded data on Titan's curious methane lakes, gathering information about potential seasons on the planet-sized moon. Then it passed through the unexplored region between Saturn itself and its famous rings. Scientists hope to learn how old the rings are and to directly examine the particles that make them up. *Cassini's* mission ended in 2017, but researchers have new questions for future exploration.

7. Which of the following best describes the organization of this passage?
   A) general-to-specific
   B) compare-contrast
   C) chronological
   D) problem-solution

The Audience

The structure, purpose, main idea, and language of a text all converge on one target: the intended **AUDIENCE**. An author makes decisions about every aspect of a piece of writing based on that audience, and readers can evaluate the writing by considering who the author is writing for. By considering the probable reactions of an intended audience, readers can determine many things:

▶ whether they are part of that intended audience

▶ the author's purpose for using specific techniques or devices

▶ the biases of the author and how they appear in the writing

▶ how the author uses rhetorical strategies.

DID YOU KNOW?
When reading a persuasive text, students should maintain awareness of what the author believes about the topic.

The audience for a text can be identified by careful analysis of the text. First, the reader considers who most likely cares about the topic and main idea of the text: who would want or need to know about this topic? The audience may be **SPECIFIC** (e.g., biologists who study sharks) or more **GENERAL** (e.g., people with an interest in marine life).

Next, consider the language of the text. The author tailors language to appeal to the intended audience, so the reader can determine from the language who the author is speaking to. A **FORMAL** style is used in business and academic settings and can make the author seem more credible. Characteristics of a formal style include:

▶ third person perspective (i.e., no use of *I* or *you*)

▶ no use of slang or clichés

▶ follows a clear structure (e.g., an introduction, a body, and a conclusion)

▶ technically correct grammar and sentence structure

▶ objective language

An INFORMAL style is used to appeal to readers in a more casual setting, such as a magazine or blog. Using an informal style may make the author seem less credible, but it can help create an emotional connection with the audience. Characteristics of informal writing include:

▶ use of first or second person (e.g., *I* or *you*)

▶ use of slang or casual language

▶ follows an unusual or flexible structure

▶ bends the rules of grammar

▶ appeals to audience's emotions

EXAMPLE

What do you do with plastic bottles? Do you throw them away, or do you recycle or reuse them? As landfills continue to fill up, there will eventually be no place to put our trash. If you recycle or reuse bottles, you will help reduce waste and turn something old into a creative masterpiece!

8. Which of the following BEST describes the intended audience for this passage?

A) a formal audience of engineering professionals

B) an audience of English language learners

C) a general audience that includes children

D) a group of scientists at an environmental conference

Evaluating Arguments

An author selects details to help support the main idea. The reader must then evaluate these details for relevance and consistency. Though the author generally includes details that support the text's main idea, it's up to the reader to decide whether those details are convincing.

Readers should be able to differentiate between facts and opinions in order to more effectively analyze supporting details. FACTS are based in truth and can usually be proven. They are pieces of information that have been confirmed or validated. An opinion is a judgment, belief, or viewpoint that is not based on evidence. OPINIONS are often stated in descriptive, subjective language that is difficult to define or prove. While opinions can be included in informative texts, they are often of little impact unless they are supported by some kind of evidence.

Sometimes, the author's BIAS—an inclination towards a particular belief—causes the author to leave out details that do not directly support the main idea or that support

QUICK REVIEW

Which of the following phrases would be associated with opinions? *for example, studies have shown, I believe, in fact, it's possible that* an opposite idea. The reader has to be able to notice not only what the author says but also what the author leaves out. Discovering the author's bias and how the supporting details reveal that bias is also key to understanding a text.

Writers will often use specific techniques, or RHETORICAL STRATEGIES, to build an argument. Readers can identify these strategies in order to clearly understand what an author wants them to believe, how the author's perspective and purpose may lead to bias, and whether the passage includes any logical fallacies.

Common rhetorical strategies include the appeals to ethos, logos, and pathos. An author uses these to build trust with the reader, explain the logical points of his or her argument, and convince the reader that his or her opinion is the best option.

An ETHOS (ETHICAL) APPEAL uses balanced, fair language and seeks to build a trusting relationship between the author and the reader. An author might explain her or his credentials, include the reader in an argument, or offer concessions to an opposing argument.

QUICK REVIEW
Consider how different audiences would react to the same text.

A LOGOS (LOGICAL) APPEAL builds on that trust by providing facts and support for the author's opinion, explaining the argument with clear connections and reasoning. At this point, the reader should beware of logical fallacies that connect unconnected ideas and build arguments on incorrect premises. With a logical appeal, an author strives to convince the reader to accept an opinion or belief by demonstrating that not only is it the most logical option but that it also satisfies her or his emotional reaction to a topic.

A PATHOS (EMOTIONAL) APPEAL does not depend on reasonable connections between ideas; rather, it seeks to remind the reader, through imagery, strong language, and personal connections, that the author's argument aligns with her or his best interests.

EXAMPLE

Exercise is critical for healthy development in children. Today in the United States, there is an epidemic of poor childhood health; many of these children will face further illnesses in adulthood that are due to poor diet and lack of exercise now. This is a problem for all Americans, especially with the rising cost of health care.

It is vital that school systems and parents encourage children to engage in a minimum of thirty minutes of cardiovascular exercise each day, mildly increasing their heart rate for a sustained period. This is proven to decrease the likelihood of developmental diabetes, obesity, and a multitude of other health problems. Also, children need a proper diet, rich in fruits and vegetables, so they can develop physically and learn healthy eating habits early on.

9. Which of the following statements from the passage is a fact, not an opinion?

A) Fruits and vegetables are the best way to help children be healthy.

B) Children today are lazier than they were in previous generations.

C) The risk of diabetes in children is reduced by physical activity.

D) Children should engage in thirty minutes of exercise a day.

Drawing Conclusions

Reading text begins with making sense of the explicit meanings of information or a narrative. Understanding occurs as the reader draws conclusions and makes logical inferences. First, the reader considers the details or facts. He or she then comes to a **CONCLUSION**—the next logical point in the thought sequence. For example, in a Hemingway story, an old man sits alone in a cafe. A young waiter says that the cafe is closing, but the old man continues to drink. The waiter starts closing up, and the old man signals for a refill. Based on these details, the reader might conclude that the old man has not understood the young waiter's desire for him to leave.

DID YOU KNOW?
When considering a character's motivations, the reader should ask what the character wants to achieve, what the character will get by accomplishing this, and what the character seems to value the most.

An inference is distinguished from a conclusion drawn. An **INFERENCE** is an assumption the reader makes based on details in the text as well as his or her own knowledge. It is more of an educated guess that extends the literal meaning of a text. Inferences begin with the given details; however, the reader uses the facts to determine additional information. What the reader already knows informs what is being suggested by the details of decisions or situations in the text. Returning to the example of the Hemingway story, the reader might *infer* that the old man is lonely, enjoys being in the cafe, and therefore is reluctant to leave.

When reading fictional text, inferring character motivations is essential. The actions of the characters move the plot forward; a series of events is understood by making sense of why the characters did what they did. Hemingway includes contrasting details as the young waiter and an older waiter discuss the old man. The older waiter sympathizes with the old man; both men have no one at home and experience a sense of emptiness in life, which motivates them to seek the cafe.

DID YOU KNOW?
Conclusions are drawn by thinking about how the author wants the reader to feel. A group of carefully selected facts can cause the reader to feel a certain way.

Another aspect of understanding text is connecting it to other texts. Readers may connect the Hemingway story about the old man in the cafe to other Hemingway stories about individuals struggling to deal with loss and loneliness in a dignified way.

They can extend their initial connections to people they know or their personal experiences. When readers read a persuasive text, they often connect the arguments made to counterarguments and opposing evidence of which they are aware. They use these connections to infer meaning.

EXAMPLE

After World War I, political and social forces pushed for a return to normalcy in the United States. The result was disengagement from the larger world and increased focus on American economic growth and personal enjoyment. Caught in the middle were American writers, raised on the values of the prewar world and frustrated with what they viewed as the superficiality and materialism of postwar American culture. Many of them fled to Paris, where they became known as the "lost generation," creating a trove of literary works criticizing their home culture and delving into their own feelings of alienation.

10. Which conclusion about the effects of war is most likely true, according to the passage?
A) War served as an inspiration for literary works.
B) It was difficult to stabilize countries after war occurred.
C) Writers were torn between supporting war and their own ideals.
D) Individual responsibility and global awareness declined after the war.

Tone and Mood

The **TONE** of a passage describes the author's attitude toward the topic. In general, the author's tone can be described as positive, negative, or neutral. The **MOOD** is the pervasive feeling or atmosphere in a passage that provokes specific emotions in the reader. Put simply, tone is how the author feels about the topic. Mood is how the reader feels about the text.

DICTION, or word choice, helps determine mood and tone in a passage. Many readers make the mistake using the author's ideas alone to determine tone; a much better practice is to look at specific words and try to identify a pattern in the emotion they evoke. Does the writer choose positive words like *ambitious* and *confident*? Or does he describe those concepts with negative words like *greedy* and *overbearing*? The first writer's tone might be described as admiring, while the more negative tone would be disapproving.

When looking at tone, it's important to examine not just the literal definition of words. Every word has not only a literal meaning but also a **CONNOTATIVE MEANING**, which relies on the common emotions and experiences an audience might associate with that word. The following words are all synonyms: *dog, puppy, cur, mutt,*

DID YOU KNOW?
To decide the connotation of a word, the reader examines whether the word conveys a positive or negative association in the mind. Adjectives are often used to influence the feelings of the reader, such as in the phrase *an ambitious attempt to achieve.*

canine, *pet*. Two of these words—*dog* and *canine*—are neutral words, without strong associations or emotions. Two others—*pet* and *puppy*—have positive associations. The last two—*cur* and *mutt*—have negative associations. A passage that uses one pair of these words versus another pair activates the positive or negative reactions of the audience.

Table 1.1. Words That Describe Tone

POSITIVE	NEUTRAL	NEGATIVE
admiring	casual	angry
approving	detached	annoyed
celebratory	formal	belligerent
earnest	impartial	bitter
encouraging	informal	condescending
excited	objective	confused
funny	questioning	cynical
hopeful	unconcerned	depressed
humorous		disrespectful
nostalgic		embarrassed
optimistic		fearful
playful		gloomy
poignant		melancholy
proud		mournful
relaxed		pessimistic
respectful		skeptical
sentimental		solemn
silly		suspicious
sympathetic		unsympathetic

EXAMPLES

Day had broken cold and grey, exceedingly cold and grey, when the man turned aside from the main Yukon trail and climbed the high earth-bank, where a dim and little-travelled trail led eastward through the fat spruce timberland. It was a steep bank, and he paused for breath at the top, excusing the act to himself by looking at his watch. It was nine o'clock. There was no sun nor hint of sun, though there was not a cloud in the sky. It was a clear day, and yet there seemed an intangible pall over the face of things, a subtle gloom that made the day dark, and that was due to the absence of sun. This fact did not worry the man. He was used to the lack of sun. It had been days since he had seen the sun, and he knew that a few more days must pass before that cheerful orb, due south, would just peep above the sky-line and dip immediately from view.

—from "To Build a Fire" by Jack London

11. Which of the following best describes the mood of the passage?

    A) exciting and adventurous

    B) unhappy and anxious

    C) bleak but accepting

    D) grim yet hopeful

12. The connotation of the words *intangible pall* is

    A) a death-like covering.

    B) a sense of familiarity.

    C) a feeling of communal strength.

    D) an understanding of the struggle ahead.

Meaning of Words and Phrases

The GED does not specifically ask you to define words, but it is good to know strategies to determine the meaning of unfamiliar words you may encounter when analyzing reading passages and improving paragraphs.

When confronted with unfamiliar words, the passage itself can help clarify their meaning. Often, identifying the tone or main idea of the passage can help eliminate answer choices. For example, if the tone of the passage is generally positive, try eliminating the answer choices with a negative connotation. Or, if the passage is about a particular occupation, rule out words unrelated to that topic.

Passages may also provide specific context clues that can help determine the meaning of a word. One type of context clue is a DEFINITION, or DESCRIPTION, CLUE. Sometimes, authors use a difficult word, then include *that is* or *which is* to signal that they are providing a definition. An author also may provide a synonym or restate the idea in more familiar words:

> Teachers often prefer teaching students with intrinsic motivation; these students have an internal desire to learn.

The meaning of *intrinsic* is restated as *an internal desire*.

Similarly, authors may include an EXAMPLE CLUE, providing an example phrase that clarifies the meaning of the word:

> Teachers may view extrinsic rewards as efficacious; however, an individual student may not be interested in what the teacher offers. For example, a student who does not like sweets may not feel any incentive to work when offered a sugary reward.

Efficacious is explained with an example that demonstrates how an extrinsic reward may not be effective.

Another commonly used context clue is the **CONTRAST**, or **ANTONYM, CLUE**. In this case, authors indicate that the unfamiliar word is the opposite of a familiar word:

> In contrast to intrinsic motivation, extrinsic motivation is contingent on teachers offering rewards that are appealing.

The phrase *in contrast* tells the reader that extrinsic is the opposite of intrinsic.

EXAMPLES

13. Which of the following is the meaning of *incentivize* as used in the sentence?

    One challenge of teaching is finding ways to incentivize, or to motivate, learning.

    A) encourage

    B) determine

    C) challenge

    D) improve

14. Which of the following is the meaning of *apprehensive* as used in the sentence?

    If an extrinsic reward is extremely desirable, a student may become so apprehensive he or she cannot focus. The student may experience such intense pressure to perform that the reward undermines its intent.

    A) uncertain

    B) distracted

    C) anxious

    D) forgetful

Figurative Language

Figures of speech are expressions that are understood to have a nonliteral meaning. Rather than stating their ideas directly, authors use **FIGURATIVE LANGUAGE** to suggest meaning by speaking of a subject as if it were something else. For example, when Shakespeare says, "All the world's a stage,/ And all men and women merely players," he is speaking of the world as if it is a stage. Since the world is not literally a stage, the reader has to ask how the two are similar and what Shakespeare might be implying about the world through this comparison. Figures of speech extend the meaning of words by engaging the reader's imagination and adding emphasis to different aspects of their subject.

A **METAPHOR** is a type of figurative language that describes something that may be unfamiliar to the reader (the topic) by referring to it as though it were something else that is more familiar to the reader (the vehicle). A metaphor stands in as a synonym, interchangeable with its corresponding topic. As the reader reflects on the similarities between the topic and the vehicle, he or she forms a clearer understanding of the topic. For example, in Shakespeare's *Romeo and Juliet*, Romeo says that "Juliet is the sun." By making this comparison, Romeo is comparing Juliet's energy to the brightness of the sun, which is familiar to readers.

A SIMILE is a type of figurative language that directly points to similarities between two things. As with a metaphor, the author uses a familiar vehicle to express an idea about a less familiar topic. Unlike a metaphor, however, a simile does not replace the object with a figurative description; it compares the vehicle and topic using "like," "as," or similar words. For example, in his poem "The Rime of the Ancient Mariner," Coleridge describes his ship as "idle as a painted ship/ Upon a painted ocean." He speaks about the boat as if it were painted (unlike Romeo above, who says explicitly that Juliet is the sun itself). The reader understands that paintings do not move, so Coleridge uses this comparison to show the reader that the ship in the poem is completely motionless.

IMAGERY is vivid description that appeals to the reader's sense of sight, sound, smell, taste, or touch. This type of figurative language allows readers to experience through their senses what is being described; as readers use their imaginations to visualize or recall sensory experience, they are drawn into the scene of the story or poem.

HYPERBOLE is an overstatement, an exaggeration intended to achieve a particular effect. Hyperbole can create humor or add emphasis to a text by drawing the reader's attention to a particular idea. For example, a character might say he or she is "so hungry, [he or she] could eat a horse." Though the character probably cannot literally eat a horse, the reader understands that he or she is extremely hungry.

PERSONIFICATION is a type of figurative language in which human characteristics are attributed to objects, abstract ideas, natural forces, or animals. For example, if a writer refers to "murmuring pine trees," he or she is attributing to the pine trees the human ability of murmuring. The writer is using the familiar vehicle of the sound of murmuring to help the reader understand the sound pine trees make in the wind.

SYMBOLISM is a literary device in which the author uses a concrete object, action, or character to represent an abstract idea. The significance of the symbol reaches beyond the object's ordinary meaning. Familiar symbols are roses representing beauty, light representing truth, and darkness representing evil. As readers notice an author's use of symbolism, they begin to make connections and to formulate ideas about what the author is suggesting.

An ALLUSION, not to be confused with illusion, is a reference to a historical person or event, a fictional character or event, a mythological or religious character or event, or an artist or artistic work. When a reader recognizes an allusion, he or she may make associations that contribute to his or her understanding of the text. For example, if a character is described as having a "Mona Lisa smile," an instant image will arise in the minds of most readers. Because allusions can be difficult to recognize, especially for young readers whose experiences are limited, teachers must provide instruction in how to recognize, research, and interpret unfamiliar references.

CLICHÉS are common sayings that lack originality but are familiar and relatable to an audience. Though clichés are not necessarily beneficial to the author who is trying to write a wholly original work, they can be helpful for a writer who is attempting to show that he or she can relate to the audience.

DIALECT and **SLANG** are linguistic qualities that an author might incorporate into his or her writing in order to develop characters or setting. A character's dialect may reveal where he or she is from, while the slang he or she uses may be an indication of social, economic, and educational status.

IRONY comes in different forms. **VERBAL IRONY** is used when a character or narrator says something that is the opposite of what he or she means. **SITUATIONAL IRONY** occurs when something happens that contradicts what the audience expected to happen. **DRAMATIC IRONY** occurs when the audience knows about something of which a character or characters are not aware.

EXAMPLE

Alfie closed his eyes and took several deep breaths. He was trying to ignore the sounds of the crowd, but even he had to admit that it was hard not to notice the tension in the stadium. He could feel 50,000 sets of eyes burning through his skin—this crowd expected perfection from him. He took another breath and opened his eyes, setting his sights on the soccer ball resting peacefully in the grass. One shot, just one last shot, between his team and the championship. He didn't look up at the goalie, who was jumping nervously on the goal line just a few yards away. Afterward, he would swear he didn't remember anything between the referee's whistle and the thunderous roar of the crowd.

15. Which of the following best describes the meaning of the phrase "he could feel 50,000 sets of eyes burning through his skin"?

    A) The 50,000 people in the stadium were trying to hurt Alfie.

    B) Alfie felt uncomfortable and exposed in front of so many people.

    C) Alfie felt immense pressure from the 50,000 people watching him.

    D) The people in the stadium are warning Alfie that the field is on fire.

Graphic Sources of Information

Informational texts on the GED may be accompanied by graphic sources of information, including graphs, diagrams, or photographs. There's no simple set of rules for handling these questions, but many of the same strategies that are used for other figures and for text passages are applicable.

Always start with the TITLE of a figure—it will provide information that is likely crucial to understanding the figure. An anatomical diagram might have a title such as *Lobes of the Brain* that tells the viewer that the diagram will likely show the names and locations of the brain's lobes. Similarly, a graph may have a title like *Number of Customers per Month*, which describes the information in the graph.

Also make sure to examine any LABELS, legends, or scales provided with the figure. Graphs, for example, should always include labels on the axes that describe what's shown on each axis, and a flowchart will have arrows indicating an ordered sequence.

Many of the strategies needed to interpret traditional reading passages can also be used for graphic representations of information, particularly those that may be text heavy. When looking at a photograph or advertisement, it will help to identify:

► the purpose of the author

► the intended audience

► rhetorical strategies designed to influence the viewer

► the main idea of the image

A flyer for a local bake sale, for example, may be designed to appeal to the viewer's emotions by including pictures of local schoolchildren. Similarly, a computer advertisement meant to appeal to corporate buyers would probably use more formal language than one aimed at teenagers.

EXAMPLE

As you can see from the graph, my babysitting business has been really successful. The year started with a busy couple of months—several snows combined with a large number of requests for Valentine's Day services boosted our sales quite a bit. The spring months have admittedly been a bit slow, but we're hoping for a big summer once school gets out. Several clients have already put in requests for our services!

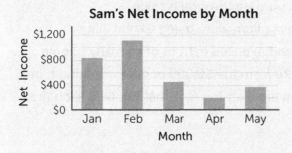

16. Based on the information in the graph, how much more did Sam's Babysitting Service bring in during February than during April?

A) $200

B) $900

C) $1100

D) $1300

Elements of Fiction

FICTION is a prose genre, made up of narratives whose details are not based in truth but are instead the creation of the author. Just as artists have the tools of color and shape to communicate ideas, so have writers their literary tools. These tools include point of view, plot, setting, character, tone, and figurative language. Each of these elements contributes to the overall idea that is developed in the text and, as such, can provide valuable insight into the theme of the work.

POINT OF VIEW is the perspective from which the action in a story is told. By carefully selecting a particular point of view, writers are able to control what their readers know. Most literature is written in either first person or third person point of view. With the FIRST PERSON POINT OF VIEW, the action is narrated by a character within the story, which can make it feel more believable and authentic to the reader. However, as a result of the first person point of view, the reader's knowledge and understanding are constrained by what the narrator notices and influenced by what the narrator thinks and values.

An author may, on the other hand, choose to tell the story from the THIRD PERSON POINT OF VIEW. A third person narrator is a voice outside the action of the story, an observer who shares what he or she knows, sees, or hears with the reader. A third person narrator might be FULLY OMNISCIENT (able to see into the minds of the characters and share what they are thinking and feeling), PARTIALLY OMNISCIENT (able to see into the minds of just one or a few characters), or LIMITED (unable to see into the minds of any of the characters and only able to share what can be seen and heard).

PLOT STRUCTURE is the way the author arranges the events of a narrative. In a conventional plot line, the story is structured around a central conflict, a struggle between two opposing forces. Conflicts in literature can be categorized in general terms as either internal or external, though most stories have a combination of both. Internal conflicts take place inside the main character's mind; he or she might be making a difficult decision, struggling with change, or sorting out priorities. External conflicts, on the other hand, occur when a character is in conflict with something or someone in the external world—the elements of nature, another character, supernatural forces, destiny, or society.

In a traditional plot structure, the author begins with EXPOSITION: important background information about the setting, the characters, and the current state of the world. Following the exposition, an INCITING INCIDENT introduces the antagonist and establishes the conflict. As the story progresses, the conflict becomes more complicated and tension increases, moving the story toward a CLIMAX or turning point, in which the conflict reaches a crisis point. Finally, there is a RESOLUTION to the conflict, followed by falling actions, events that move the characters away from the conflict and into a new life.

SETTING is the geographical and chronological location of events in a story. When considering setting, readers should examine how characters interact with their surroundings, how they are influenced by the societal expectations of that time and place, and how the location and time period impact the development of the story. Often, setting can seem inseparable from plot; therefore, a helpful question for beginning the discussion of setting is, How would this story change if it were set in a different time or place?

CHARACTER DEVELOPMENT is the process an author uses to create characters that are complex and, to some degree, believable. One way authors develop their characters is directly: they tell the reader explicitly what the character is like by describing traits and assigning values. Sometimes, authors might include the thoughts and feelings of the characters themselves, offering readers even more insight. Authors can also develop their characters indirectly by revealing their actions and interactions with others, sometimes including what one character says or thinks about another and allowing the reader to draw his or her own conclusions. Most authors use a combination of direct and indirect characterization; this ensures that readers know what they need to know while also providing opportunities for reflection and interpretation.

EXAMPLE

17. Which passage below from *A Mystery of Heroism* by Stephen Crane best demonstrates the third person omniscient point of view?

A) In the midst of it all Smith and Ferguson, two privates of A Company, were engaged in a heated discussion, which involved the greatest questions of the national existence.

B) An officer screamed out an order so violently that his voice broke and ended the sentence in a falsetto shriek.

C) The officer's face was grimy and perspiring, and his uniform was tousled as if he had been in direct grapple with an enemy. He smiled grimly when the men stared at him.

D) No, it could not be true. He was not a hero. Heroes had no shames in their lives, and, as for him, he remembered borrowing fifteen dollars from a friend and promising to pay it back the next day, and then avoiding that friend for ten months.

Test Your Knowledge

Read each passage, and then choose the most correct answer.

1. The cisco, a foot-long freshwater fish native to the Great Lakes, once thrived throughout the basin but had virtually disappeared by the 1950s. However, today fishermen are pulling them up by the net-load in Lake Michigan and Lake Ontario. It is highly unusual for a native species to revive, and the reason for the cisco's reemergence is even more unlikely. The cisco have an invasive species, quagga mussels, to thank for their return. Quagga mussels depleted nutrients in the lakes, harming other species highly dependent on these nutrients. Cisco, however, thrive in low-nutrient environments. As other species—many invasive—diminished, cisco flourished in their place.

    It can be inferred from the passage that most invasive species

    A) support the growth of native species.

    B) do not impact the development of native species.

    C) struggle to survive in their new environments.

    D) cause the decline of native species.

2. When a fire destroyed San Francisco's American Indian Center in October of 1969, American Indian groups set their sights on the recently closed island prison of Alcatraz as a site of a new Indian cultural center and school. Ignored by the government, an activist group known as Indians of All Tribes sailed to Alcatraz in the early morning hours with eighty-nine men, women, and children. They landed on Alcatraz, claiming it for all the tribes of North America. Their demands were ignored, and so the group continued to occupy the island for the next nineteen months, its numbers swelling up to 600 as others joined. By January of 1970, many of the original protestors had left, and on June 11, 1971, federal marshals forcibly removed the last residents.

    The main idea of this passage is that

    A) the government refused to listen to the demands of American Indians.

    B) American Indians occupied Alcatraz in protest of government policy.

    C) few people joined the occupation of Alcatraz, weakening its effectiveness.

    D) the government took violent action against protestors at Alcatraz.

3. Archaeologists have discovered the oldest known specimens of bedbugs in a cave in Oregon where humans once lived. The three different species date back to between 5,000 and 11,000 years ago. The finding gives scientists a clue as to how bedbugs became human parasites. These bedbugs, like those that plague humans today, originated as bat parasites. Scientists hypothesize that it was the co-habitation of humans and bats in the caves that encouraged the bugs to begin feeding on the humans. The three species found in the Oregon caves are actually still around today, although they continue to prefer bats. Humans only lived seasonally in the Oregon cave

system, however, which might explain why these insects did not fully transfer to human hosts like bedbugs elsewhere did.

With which of the following claims about bedbugs would the author most likely agree?

A) Modern bedbugs that prefer humans thrive better in areas with extensive light.

B) Bedbugs are a relatively fragile species that has struggled to survive over time.

C) The transition to humans significantly accelerated the growth of bedbug populations.

D) Bedbugs that prefer humans originated in caves that humans occupied year-round.

4. In a remote nature preserve in northeastern Siberia, scientists are attempting to recreate the subarctic steppe grassland ecosystem that flourished there during the last Ice Age. The area today is dominated by forests, but the lead scientists of the project believe the forested terrain was neither a natural development nor environmentally advantageous. They believe that if they can restore the grassland, they will be able to slow climate change by slowing the thawing of the permafrost which lies beneath the tundra. Key to this undertaking is restoring the wildlife to the region, including wild horses, musk oxen, bison, and yak. Most ambitiously, the scientists hope to revive the wooly mammoth species which was key in trampling the ground and knocking down the trees, helping to keep the land free for grasses to grow.

    In the second sentence, the word *advantageous* most nearly means

    A) beneficial

    B) damaging

    C) useful

    D) appropriate

5. The heart works by shifting between two states: systole and diastole. In systole, the cardiac muscles are contracting and moving blood from any given chamber. During diastole, the muscles are relaxing and the chamber is expanding to fill with blood. The systole and diastole are responsible blood pressure—the pressure in the major arteries. This is the blood pressure that is measured in a regular exam. The two values are systolic and diastolic pressures, respectively. Because it is measured when blood is being pumped into the arteries, systolic blood pressure is always the higher number.

    Systolic blood pressure is correlated with negative health outcomes such as stroke and heart failure. For this reason, doctor's categorize patients based on their systolic blood pressure. These categories are given below.

Categories	Systolic Range
Normal	< 120
Prehypertension	120 – 139
Hypertension Stage 1	140 – 159
Hypertension Stage 2	160 – 179
Hypertensive Crisis	> 180

If a person has a blood pressure of 151/95, which category would their doctor place them in?

A) normal

B) prehypertension

C) hypertension stage 1

D) hypertension stage 2

6. The odds of success for any new restaurant are slim. Competition in the city is fierce, and the low margin of return means that aspiring restaurateurs must be exact and ruthless with their budget and pricing. The fact that The City Café has lasted as long as it has is a testament to its owners' skills.

Which of the following conclusions is well supported by the passage?

A) The City Café offers the best casual dining in town.

B) The City Café has a well-managed budget and prices items on its menu appropriately.

C) The popularity of The City Café will likely fall as new restaurants open in the city.

D) The City Café has a larger margin of return than other restaurants in the city.

7. The social and political discourse of America continues to be permeated with idealism. An idealistic viewpoint asserts that the ideals of freedom, equality, justice, and human dignity are the truths that Americans must continue to aspire to. Idealists argue that truth is what should be, not necessarily what is. In general, they work to improve things and to make them as close to ideal as possible.

The purpose of the passage is to

A) advocate for freedom, equality, justice, and human rights

B) explain what an idealist believes in

C) explain what's wrong with social and political discourse in America

D) persuade readers to believe in certain truths

8. Alexander Hamilton and James Madison called for the Constitutional Convention to write a constitution as the foundation of a stronger federal government. Madison and other Federalists like John Adams believed in separation of powers, republicanism, and a strong federal government. Despite the separation of powers that would be provided for in the US Constitution, anti-Federalists like Thomas Jefferson called for even more limitations on the power of the federal government.

   In the context of the passage above, which of the following would most likely NOT support a strong federal government?

   A) Alexander Hamilton

   B) James Madison

   C) John Adams

   D) Thomas Jefferson

9. It's that time again—the annual Friendswood Village Summer Fair is here! Last year we had a record number of visitors, and we're expecting an even bigger turnout this year. The fair will be bringing back all our traditional food and games, including the famous raffle. This year, we'll have a carousel, petting zoo, and climbing wall (for teenagers and adults only, please). We're also excited to welcome Petey's BBQ and Happy Tummy's Frozen Treats, who are both new to the fair this year. Tickets are available online and at local retailers.

   Which of the following will NOT be a new presence at the Fair this year?

   A) the raffle

   B) the petting zoo

   C) the carousel

   D) the climbing wall

10. After looking at five houses, Robert and I have decided to buy the one on Forest Road. The first two homes we visited didn't have the space we need—the first had only one bathroom, and the second did not have a guest bedroom. The third house, on Pine Street, had enough space inside but didn't have a big enough yard for our three dogs. The fourth house we looked at, on Rice Avenue, was stunning but well above our price range. The last home, on Forest Road, wasn't in the neighborhood we wanted to live in. However, it had the right amount of space for the right price.

    What is the author's conclusion about the house on Pine Street?

    A) The house did not have enough bedrooms.

    B) The house did not have a big enough yard.

    C) The house was not in the right neighborhood.

    D) The house was too expensive.

11. The study showed that private tutoring is providing a significant advantage to those students who are able to afford it. Researchers looked at the grades of students who had received free tutoring through the school versus those whose parents had paid for private tutors. The study included 2500 students in three high schools across four grade levels. The study found that private tutoring corresponded with a rise in grade point average (GPA) of 0.5 compared to students who used the school's free tutor service and 0.7 compared to students who used no tutoring. After reviewing the study, the board is recommending that the school restructure its free tutor service to provide a more equitable education for all students.

Which of the following would weaken the author's argument?

A) the fact that the cited study was funded by a company that provides discounted tutoring through schools

B) a study showing differences in standardized test scores between students at schools in different neighborhoods

C) a statement signed by local teachers stating that they do not provide preferential treatment in the classroom or when grading

D) a study showing that GPA does not strongly correlate with success in college

12. It could be said that the great battle between the North and South we call the Civil War was a battle for individual identity. The states of the South had their own culture, one based on farming, independence, and the rights of both man and state to determine their own paths. Similarly, the North had forged its own identity as a center of centralized commerce and manufacturing. This clash of lifestyles was bound to create tension, and this tension was bound to lead to war. But people who try to sell you this narrative are wrong. The Civil War was not a battle of cultural identities—it was a battle about slavery. All other explanations for the war are either a direct consequence of the South's desire for wealth at the expense of her fellow man or a fanciful invention to cover up this sad portion of our nation's history. And it cannot be denied that this time in our past was very sad indeed.

The purpose of the passage is to

A) convince readers that slavery was the main cause of the Civil War

B) illustrate the cultural differences between the North and the South before the Civil War

C) persuade readers that the North deserved to win the Civil War

D) demonstrate that the history of the Civil War is too complicated to be understood clearly

13. East River High School has released its graduation summary for the class of 2016. Out of a total of 558 senior students, 525 (94 percent) successfully completed their degree program and graduated. Of these, 402 (representing

72 percent of the total class) went on to attend to a two- or four-year college or university. The distribution of students among the four main types of colleges and universities—small or large private and small or large public—is shown in the figure below. As the data shows, the majority of East River High School's college-attending graduates chose a large, public institution.

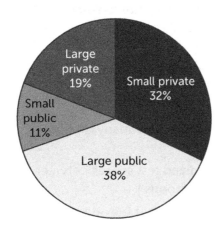

According to the figure, how many students from East River High School will attend a small, public college or university?

A) 4

B) 44

C) 440

D) 4400

14. The Gatling gun, a forerunner of the modern machine gun, was an early rapid-fire spring loaded, hand-cranked weapon. In 1861, Dr. Richard J. Gatling designed the gun to allow one person to fire many shots quickly. His goal was to reduce the death toll of war by decreasing the number of soldiers needed to fight. The gun consisted of a central shaft surrounded by six rotating barrels. A soldier turned a crank which rotated the shaft. As each barrel reached a particular point in the cycle, it fired, ejected its spent cartridge and loaded another. During this process, it cooled down, preparing it to fire again. The Gatling gun was first used in combat by the Union Army during the Civil War. However, each gun was purchased directly by individual commanders. The US Army did not purchase a Gatling gun until 1866.

The purpose of the passage is to

A) explain why the Gatling gun was harmful to troops.

B) critique the US Army's use of the Gatling gun.

C) describe the design and early history of the Gatling gun.

D) analyze the success of Dr. Gatling in achieving his goals.

15.

> Alan —
>
> I just wanted to drop you a quick note to let you know I'll be out of the office for the next two weeks. Elizabeth and I are finally taking that trip to France we've been talking about for years. It's a bit of a last-minute decision, but since we had the vacation time available, we figured it was now or never.
>
> Anyway, my team's been briefed on the upcoming meeting, so they should be able to handle the presentation without any hiccups. If you have any questions or concerns, you can direct them to Joanie, who'll be handling my responsibilities while I'm out.
>
> Let me know if you want any special treats. I don't know if you can take chocolate and cheese on the plane, but I'm going to try!
>
> Best regards,
>
> Michael

Which of the following best describes the writer's tone?

A) competitive

B) formal

C) friendly

D) caring

Questions 16–20 are based on the following passage.

The bacteria, fungi, insects, plants, and animals that live together in a habitat have evolved to share a pool of limited resources. They've competed for water, minerals, nutrients, sunlight, and space—sometimes for thousands or even millions of years. As these communities have evolved, the species in them have developed complex, long-term interspecies interactions known as symbiotic relationships.

Ecologists characterize these interactions based on whether each party benefits. In mutualism, both individuals benefit, while in synnecrosis, both organisms are harmed. A relationship where one individual benefits and the other is harmed is known as parasitism. Examples of these relationships can easily be seen in any ecosystem. Pollination, for example, is mutualistic—pollinators get nutrients from the flower, and the plant is able to reproduce—while tapeworms, which steal nutrients from their host, are parasitic.

There's yet another class of symbiosis that is <u>controversial</u> among scientists. As it's long been defined, commensalism is a relationship where one species benefits and the other is unaffected. But is it possible for two species to interact and for one to remain completely unaffected? Often, relationships described as commensal include one species that feeds on another species' leftovers; remoras, for instance, will attach themselves to sharks and eat the food particles they leave behind. It might seem like the shark gets nothing from the relationship, but a closer look will show that sharks in fact benefit from remoras, which clean the sharks' skin and remove parasites. In fact, many scientists claim that relationships currently described as commensal are just mutualistic or parasitic in ways that haven't been discovered yet.

16. What is the meaning of the word *controversial* in the last paragraph?
    A) debatable
    B) disbelieved
    C) confusing
    D) upsetting

17. The purpose of the passage is to
    A) argue that commensalism isn't actually found in nature
    B) describe the many types of symbiotic relationships
    C) explain how competition for resources results in long-term interspecies relationships
    D) provide examples of the many different ways individual organisms interact

18. Which of the following is NOT a fact stated in the passage?
    A) Mutualism is an interspecies relationship where both species benefit.
    B) Synnecrosis is an interspecies relationship where both species are harmed.
    C) The relationship between plants and pollinators is mutualistic.
    D) The relationship between remoras and sharks is parasitic.

19. Epiphytes are plants that attach themselves to trees and derive nutrients from the air and surrounding debris. Sometimes, the weight of epiphytes can damage the trees on which they're growing. The relationship between epiphytes and their hosts would be described as _____.
    A) mutualism
    B) commensalism
    C) parasitism
    D) synnecrosis

20. What can the reader conclude from this passage about symbiotic relationships?
    A) Scientists cannot decide how to classify symbiotic relationships among species.
    B) The majority of interspecies interactions are parasitic because most species do not get along.
    C) If two species are involved in a parasitic relationship, one of the species will eventually become extinct.
    D) Symbiotic relationships evolve as the species that live in a community adapt to their environments and each other.

Answer Key
EXAMPLES

1. **D) is correct.** The art of the modern period reflects the new technologies and globalization possible through the internet.

2. **A) is correct.** According to the text, technology and the internet have "diversified the art world and brought it together simultaneously."

3. **B) is correct.** This option indicates both the main idea and what the reader will focus on while reading.

4. **D) is correct.** The phrase "no shortage of things to do or sights to see" suggests the writer is enthusiastic about the many interesting activities possible in California. There is no indication that the writer should do everything, though, or that one part is better than another.

5. **C) is correct.** The passage states that hiring subcontractors provides the advantage of "reduced legal responsibility to employees."

6. **D) is correct.** The text provides details on the experiment as well as its results.

7. **C) is correct.** The passage describes the journey of Cassini in chronological order: it passed by Titan, went through the region between Saturn and its rings, and ended its mission in 2017.

8. **C) is correct.** The informal tone and direct address of this passage suggest that the author is writing for a general audience that may include children. For instance, turning bottles into an art project could be a good activity for children.

9. **C) is correct.** Choice C is a simple fact stated by the author. It is introduced by the word *proven* to indicate that it is supported by evidence.

10. **D) is correct.** After the war, in the US there was a lack of focus on the world and greater focus on personal comforts, which writers viewed as superficiality and materialism.

11. **C) is correct.** The day is described as "cold and grey" with an "intangible pall," which creates a bleak mood. However, the man himself "did not worry" and knew that only "a few more days must pass" before he would see the sun again, suggesting he has accepted his circumstances.

12. **A) is correct.** Within the context of the sentence "It was a clear day, and yet there seemed an intangible pall over the face of things, a subtle gloom that made the day dark," the words *gloom* and *dark* are suggestive of death; the phrase *over the face* suggests a covering.

13. **A) is correct.** The word *incentivize* is defined immediately with the synonym *motivate*, or *encourage*.

14. **C) is correct.** The reader can infer that the *pressure to perform* is making the student anxious.

15. **C) is correct.** The metaphor implies that Alfie felt pressure from the people watching him to perform well. There is no indication that he is threatened physically.

16. **B) is correct.** In February the service earned $1100, and in April it earned $200. The difference between the two months is $900.

17. **D) is correct.** The narrator is reporting the thoughts of the character, as the character's memory about not acting heroic in the past is revealed. The other choices only include descriptions of the characters words or actions.

TEST YOUR KNOWLEDGE

1. **D) is correct.** The author writes that "the reason for the cisco's reemergence is even more unlikely. The cisco have an invasive species, quagga mussels, to thank for their return."

2. **B) is correct.** The author states, "Ignored by the government, an activist group known as Indians of All Tribes sailed to Alcatraz in the early morning hours with eighty-nine men, women, and children." The author goes on to describe the nineteen-month occupation of the island.

3. **D) is correct.** The author writes, "Humans only lived seasonally in the Oregon cave system, however, which might explain why these insects did not fully transfer to human hosts like bedbugs elsewhere did."

4. **A) is correct.** The author goes on to explain that the development of forests was not good for the environment: scientists believe grasslands would slow climate change.

5. **C) is correct.** A systolic blood pressure reading of 151 (the higher number) places the patient in the hypertension stage 1 category.

6. **B) is correct.** The passage states that restaurateurs must be "exact and ruthless with their budget and pricing." The success of The City Café implies that its owners have done that.

7. **B) is correct.** The purpose of the passage is to explain what an idealist believes in. The author does not offer any opinions or try to persuade readers about the importance of certain values.

8. **D) is correct.** In the passage, Thomas Jefferson is defined as an anti-Federalist, in contrast with Federalists who believed in a strong federal government.

9. **A) is correct.** The raffle is the only feature described as an event the organizers will be "bringing back[.]"

10. **B) is correct.** The author says that the house on Pine Street "had enough space inside but didn't have a big enough yard for [their] three dogs."

11. **A) is correct.** A company that profits from private tutoring might introduce bias into a study on the effects of private tutoring in schools.

12. **A) is correct.** The author writes, "But people who try to sell you this narrative are wrong. The Civil War was not a battle of cultural identities—it was a battle about slavery."

13. **B) is correct.** The passage states that 402 students went on to attend college or university, and 11 percent of 402 is approximately 44 students.

14. **C) is correct.** The author explains why the gun was created, how it functions, and how it was initially used.

15. **C) is correct.** The author and Alan have a friendly relationship, as evidenced by the author's informal tone and his offer to bring Alan a gift from his vacation.

16. **A) is correct.** The author writes that "[t]here's yet another class of symbiosis that is controversial among scientists" and goes on to say that "many scientists claim that relationships currently described as commensal are just mutualistic or parasitic in ways that haven't been discovered yet." This implies that scientists debate about the topic of commensalism.

17. **B) is correct.** The author writes that "[a]s these communities have evolved, the species in them have developed complex, long-term interspecies interactions known as symbiotic relationships." She then goes on to describe the different types of symbiotic relationships that exist.

18. **D) is correct.** The author writes, "Often, relationships described as commensal include one species that feeds on another species' leftovers; remoras, for instance, will attach themselves to sharks and eat the food particles they leave behind. It might seem like the shark gets nothing from the relationship, but a closer look will show that sharks in fact benefit from remoras, which clean the sharks' skin and remove parasites."

19. **C) is correct.** The author writes, "A relationship where one individual benefits and the other is harmed is known as parasitism."

20. **D) is correct.** The author writes, "The bacteria, fungi, insects, plants, and animals that live together in a habitat have evolved to share a pool of limited resources...As these communities have evolved, the species in them have developed complex, long-term interspecies interactions known as symbiotic relationships."

CHAPTER TWO
Grammar and Sentence Structure

The Reasoning Through Language Arts test of the GED will test your understanding of the basic rules of grammar. You will be asked to improve paragraphs by choosing the best way to complete sentences. To do so correctly, you must know the basic rules of grammar, mechanics, and sentence structure.

Parts of Speech

The **PARTS OF SPEECH** are the building blocks of sentences, paragraphs, and entire texts. Grammarians have typically defined eight parts of speech—nouns, pronouns, verbs, adverbs, adjectives, conjunctions, prepositions, and interjections—all of which play unique roles in the context of a sentence. Thus, a fundamental understanding of the parts of speech is necessary for comprehending basic sentence construction.

Though some words fall easily into one category or another, many words can function as different parts of speech based on their usage within a sentence.

NOUNS and PRONOUNS

NOUNS are the words that describe people, places, things, and ideas. Most often, nouns fill the position of subject or object within a sentence. Nouns have several subcategories: common nouns (*chair, car, house*), proper nouns (*Julie, David*), noncountable nouns (*money, water*), and countable nouns (*dollars, cubes*), among others. There is much crossover among these subcategories (for example, *chair* is common and countable), and other subcategories do exist.

PRONOUNS replace nouns in a sentence or paragraph, allowing a writer to achieve a smooth flow throughout a text by avoiding unnecessary repetition. While there are countless nouns in the English language, there are only a few types of pronouns. The ones important for the GED follow:

PERSONAL PRONOUNS act as subjects or objects in a sentence.

> <u>She</u> received a letter; I gave the letter to <u>her</u>.

POSSESSIVE PRONOUNS indicate possession.

> The apartment is <u>hers</u>, but the furniture is <u>mine</u>.

REFLEXIVE or **INTENSIVE PRONOUNS** intensify a noun or reflect back on a noun.

> I made the dessert <u>myself.</u>

INDEFINITE PRONOUNS simply replace nouns to avoid unnecessary repetition.

> <u>Several</u> came to the party to see <u>both</u>.

Table 2.1. Personal, Possessive, and Reflexive Pronouns

CASE	FIRST PERSON		SECOND PERSON		THIRD PERSON	
	Singular	Plural	Singular	Plural	Singular	Plural
Subject	I	we	you	you (all)	he, she, it	they
Object	me	us	you	you (all)	him, her, it	them
Possessive	mine	ours	yours	yours	his, hers, its	theirs
Reflexive/ intensive	myself	ourselves	yourself	yourselves	himself, herself, itself	themselves

EXAMPLES

1. What purpose do nouns usually serve in a sentence?
   A) They indicate possession.
   B) They act as subject or object.
   C) They intensify other nouns.
   D) They clarify when an action occurs.

2. Which pronoun best completes the sentence?
   _____ baked the cookies ourselves and ate most of them.
   A) She
   B) Her
   C) I
   D) We

VERBS

VERBS express action (*run, jump, play*) or state of being (*is, seems*). Verbs that describe action are ACTION VERBS, and those that describe being are LINKING VERBS.

> ACTION: My brother <u>plays</u> tennis.
> LINKING: He <u>is</u> the best player on the team.

Verbs are conjugated to indicate PERSON, which refers to the point of view of the sentence. First person is the speaker (*I, we*); second person is the person being addressed (*you*); and third person is outside the conversation (*they, them*). Verbs are also conjugated to match the NUMBER (singular or plural) of their subject. HELPING VERBS (*to be, to have, to do*) are used to conjugate verbs. An unconjugated verb is called an INFINITIVE and includes the word *to* in front (*to be, to break*).

PARTICIPLES are verb forms lacking number and person. The PAST PARTICIPLE is usually formed by adding the suffix *–ed* to the verb stem (*type* becomes *typed; drop* becomes *dropped*). The PRESENT PARTICIPLE is always formed by adding the suffix *–ing* to the verb stem (*typing, dropping*). Participles are used in verb conjugation to indicate the state of an action (*she is going; we had waited*).

Participles also act in *participial phrases* that act as descriptors in sentences:

> <u>Seated</u> politely, Ron listened to his friend's boring story.
> Maya petted the <u>sleeping</u> cat.

When a present participle acts as a noun, it is called a GERUND. In the following sentence, *running* is a noun and serving as the subject of the sentence:

> <u>Running</u> is my favorite form of exercise.

A common error in sentence structure is the *dangling participle*: when a participial phrase is disconnected from the word or phrase it modifies.

> INCORRECT: <u>Discussing the state of the nation</u>, I listened to the president's speech.

Here, the president, not the narrator, is discussing the state of the nation; the narrator is simply *listening*. However, the participial phrase "Discussing the state of the nation" is disconnected from the word it modifies, *president*. Thus it is *dangling* in the sentence—a dangling participle.

To fix a dangling particle, rearrange the sentence so that the modifying phrase is next to the word it modifies.

> CORRECT: I listened to the president's speech <u>discussing the state of the nation</u>.

Table 2.2. Verb Conjugation (Present Tense)

Person	Singular	Plural
First person	I give	we give
Second person	you give	you (all) give
Third person	he/she/it/ gives	they give

Verbs are also conjugated to indicate TENSE, or when the action has happened. Actions can happen in the past, present, or future. Tense also describes over how long a period the action took place:

▶ SIMPLE verbs describe something that happened once or general truths.

▶ CONTINUOUS verbs describe an ongoing action.

▶ PERFECT verbs describe repeated actions or actions that started in the past and have been completed.

▶ PERFECT CONTINUOUS verbs describe actions that started in the past and are continuing.

Table 2.3. Verb Tenses

Tense	Past	Present	Future
Simple	I gave her a gift yesterday.	I give her a gift every day.	I will give her a gift on her birthday.
Continuous	I was giving her a gift when you got here.	I am giving her a gift; come in!	I will be giving her a gift at dinner.
Perfect	I had given her a gift before you got there.	I have given her a gift already.	I will have given her a gift by midnight.
Perfect continuous	Her friends had been giving her gifts all night when I arrived.	I have been giving her gifts every year for nine years.	I will have been giving her gifts on holidays for ten years next year.

Verbs that follow the standard rules of conjugation are called REGULAR verbs. IRREGULAR verbs do not follow these rules, and their conjugations must be memorized. Some examples of irregular verbs are given in Table 2.4.

Table 2.4. Irregular Verbs

Present	Past	Has/Have/Had
am	was	been
do	did	done
see	saw	seen
write	wrote	written

PRESENT	PAST	HAS/HAVE/HAD
break	broke	broken
grow	grew	grown
speak	spoke	spoken
begin	began	begun
run	ran	run
buy	bought	bought

TRANSITIVE VERBS take a DIRECT OBJECT, which receives the action of the verb. Intransitive verbs have no object. The person or thing that receives the direct object is the INDIRECT OBJECT.

> TRANSITIVE: Alex gave the ball to his brother.
> (The *ball* is the direct object; *his* brother is the indirect object.)
> INTRANSITIVE: She jumped over the fence.

EXAMPLES

3. Which verb phrase best completes the sentence?

   By this time tomorrow, we _____ in New York.

   A) will have arrived

   B) have arrived

   C) arrive

   D) was arriving

4. Identify the direct object in the following sentence:

   My friends brought me a package of souvenirs from their trip to Spain.

   A) friends

   B) me

   C) package

   D) trip

ADJECTIVES and ADVERBS

ADJECTIVES modify or describe nouns and pronouns. In English, adjectives are usually placed before the word being modified, although they can also appear after a linking verb such as *is* or *smells*.

> The beautiful blue jade necklace will go perfectly with my dress.
> I think that lasagna smells delicious.

When multiple adjectives are used, they should be listed in the following order:

1. Determiners: articles (*a, an,* and *the*), possessive adjectives (e.g., *my, her*), and descriptors of quantity (e.g., *three, several*)

2. Opinions: modifiers that imply a value (e.g., *beautiful, perfect, ugly*)

3. Size: descriptions of size (e.g., *small, massive*)

4. Age: descriptions of age (e.g., *young, five-year-old*)

5. Shape: descriptions of appearance or character (e.g., *smooth, loud*)

6. Color: descriptions of color (e.g., *blue, dark*)

7. Origin: modifiers that describe where something came from (e.g., *American, homemade*)

8. Material: modifiers that describe what something is made from (e.g., *cotton, metallic*)

9. Purpose: adjectives that function as part of the noun to describe its purpose (e.g., <u>sewing</u> *machine,* <u>rocking</u> *chair*)

ADVERBS, which are often formed by adding the suffix *–ly,* modify any word or set of words that is not a noun or pronoun. They can modify verbs, adjectives, other adverbs, phrases, or clauses.

> He <u>quickly</u> ran to the house next door. (*Quickly* modifies the verb *ran.*)
> Her <u>very</u> effective speech earned her a promotion. (*Very* modifies the adjective *effective.*)
> <u>Finally</u>, the table was set and dinner was ready. (*Finally* modifies the clause *the table was set and dinner was ready.*)

DID YOU KNOW?
Adjectives answer the questions *what kind, how many,* or *which one?*
Adverbs answer the questions *how, when, where, why,* or *to what extent?*

COMPARATIVE adjectives and adverbs compare two items. For most one- or two-syllable words, the suffix *–er* is added to make it comparative; the word may be followed by *than.*

SUPERLATIVE adjectives and adverbs compare three or more items. Most one- or two-syllable words are made superlative by adding a suffix, *–est.*

> Comparative: My brother is <u>taller</u> than my sister.
> Superlative: My brother is the <u>tallest</u> of my five siblings.

Longer adjectives and adverbs must be preceded by *more* to form the comparative and *most* to form the superlative.

> Comparative: My bed at home is <u>more comfortable</u> than the one at the hotel.
> Superlative: The bed in your guestroom is the <u>most comfortable</u> bed I've ever slept in!

Some adjectives and adverbs form irregular comparatives and superlatives (see Table 2.5.).

> Comparative: The weather is bad today, but it was <u>worse</u> yesterday.
> Superlative: The <u>worst</u> day this week was Monday, when it rained.

Table 2.5. Irregular Comparative and Superlative Adjectives and Adverbs		
ADJECTIVE/ADVERB	COMPARATIVE	SUPERLATIVE
much	more	most
bad	worse	worst
good	better	best
little	less	least
far	further/farther	furthest/farthest

EXAMPLES

5. Which of the following sentences is CORRECTLY constructed?
    A) Between my mom and dad, my father is the oldest.
    B) I ran less than usual today.
    C) Henry's cat is more fatter than mine.
    D) After taking medicine, she felt worser.

6. Which is the adverb in the following sentence?
    He carelessly sped around the flashing yellow light.
    A) flashing
    B) yellow
    C) around
    D) carelessly

CONJUNCTIONS

CONJUNCTIONS join words into phrases, clauses, and sentences. The *coordinating conjunctions* (FANBOYS) join two independent clauses: **F**or, **A**nd, **N**or, **B**ut, **O**r, **Y**et, **S**o.

> Marta went to the pool, <u>and</u> Alex decided to go shopping.
> Aisha didn't want to eat tacos for dinner, <u>so</u> she picked up a pizza on her way home.

Subordinating conjunctions join dependent clauses to the independent clauses to which they are related.

> We chose that restaurant <u>because</u> Juan loves pizza.

Table 2.6. Subordinating Conjunctions	
Time	after, as, as long as, as soon as, before, since, until, when, whenever, while
Manner	as, as if, as though
Cause	because
Condition	although, as long as, even if, even though, if, provided that, though, unless, while
Purpose	in order that, so that, that
Comparison	as, than

EXAMPLES

7. The following sentence contains an error. How should it be rewritten?

    He liked to cook and baking was his specialty.

    A) He liked to cook, and baking was his specialty.

    B) He liked to cook so baking was his specialty.

    C) He liked to cook; and baking was his specialty.

    D) He liked to cook, baking was his specialty.

8. Identify the underlined part of speech in the following sentence:

    Anne and Peter drank their coffee languidly <u>while</u> they read the paper.

    A) subordinating conjunction

    B) coordinating conjunction

    C) irregular verb

    D) adverb

PREPOSITIONS

PREPOSITIONS set up relationships in time (*after the party*) or space (*under the cushions*) within a sentence. A preposition will always function as part of a prepositional phrase—the preposition along with the object of the preposition.

Table 2.7. Common Prepositions			
PREPOSITIONS			
about	by	off	toward
among	despite	on	under
around	down	onto	underneath
at	during	out	until
before	except	outside	up

behind	for	over	upon
below	from	past	with
beneath	in	since	within
beside	into	through	
between	near	till	
beyond	of	to	

COMPOUND PREPOSITIONS			
according to	because of	in place of	on account of
as of	by means of	in respect to	out of
as well as	in addition to	in spite of	prior to
aside from	in front of	instead of	with regard to

EXAMPLE

9. Identify the prepositional phrase in the following sentence.

   John and Carol must drive through the tunnel, but Carol is claustrophobic.

   A) must drive

   B) through the tunnel

   C) drive through

   D) but Carol is

INTERJECTIONS

INTERJECTIONS have no grammatical attachment to the sentence itself other than to add expressions of emotion. These parts of speech may be punctuated with commas or exclamation points and may fall anywhere within the sentence.

> Ouch! He stepped on my toe.

EXAMPLE

10. Identify the interjection in the following sentence.

   "Come here! Look! Our team won the Super Bowl! Yay!"

   A) Come here!

   B) Our team won

   C) Look!

   D) Yay!

Constructing Sentences
PHRASES

A PHRASE is a group of words that communicates a partial idea and lacks either a subject or a predicate. Several phrases may be strung together, one after another, to add detail and interest to a sentence.

Phrases are categorized based on the main word in the phrase. A PREPOSITIONAL PHRASE begins with a preposition and ends with an object of the preposition; a VERB PHRASE is composed of the main verb along with its helping verbs; and a NOUN PHRASE consists of a noun and its modifiers.

> PREPOSITIONAL PHRASE: The dog is hiding under the porch.
> VERB PHRASE: The chef wanted to cook a different dish.
> NOUN PHRASE: The big, red barn rests beside the vacant chicken house.

An APPOSITIVE PHRASE is a particular type of noun phrase that renames the word or group of words that precedes it. Appositive phrases usually follow the noun they describe and are set apart by commas.

> Appositive phrase: My dad, a clock maker, loved antiques.

VERBAL PHRASES begin with a word that would normally act as a verb but is instead filling another role within the sentence. These phrases can act as nouns, adjectives, or adverbs.

> NOUN: To become a doctor had always been her goal.
> ADJECTIVE: Enjoying the stars that filled the sky, Ben lingered outside for quite a while.

EXAMPLE

11. Identify the type of phrase underlined in the following sentence:

    Dodging traffic, Rachel drove to work on back roads.

    A) prepositional phrase
    B) noun phrase
    C) verb phrase
    D) verbal phrase

CLAUSES and TYPES of SENTENCES

CLAUSES contain both a subject and a predicate. They can be either independent or dependent. An INDEPENDENT (or main) CLAUSE can stand alone as its own sentence:

> The dog ate her homework.

Dependent (or subordinate) clauses cannot stand alone as their own sentences. They start with a subordinating conjunction, relative pronoun, or relative adjective, which will make them sound incomplete:

<u>Because</u> the dog ate her homework

Table 2.8. Words That Begin Dependent Clauses

Subordinating Conjunctions	Relative Pronouns and Adjectives
after, before, once, since, until, when, whenever, while, as, because, in order that, so, so that, that, if, even if, provided that, unless, although, even though, though, whereas, where, wherever, than, whether	who, whoever, whom, whomever, whose, which, that, when, where, why, how

Sentences can be classified based on the number and type of clauses they contain. A **SIMPLE SENTENCE** will have only one independent clause and no dependent clauses. The sentence may contain phrases, complements, and modifiers, but it will comprise only one independent clause, one complete idea.

The cat ran under the porch.

A **COMPOUND SENTENCE** has two or more independent clauses and no dependent clauses.

The cat ran under the porch, and the dog ran after him.

A **COMPLEX SENTENCE** has only one independent clause and one or more dependent clauses.

The cat, who is scared of the dog, ran under the porch.

A **COMPOUND-COMPLEX SENTENCE** has two or more independent clauses and one or more dependent clauses.

The cat, who is scared of the dog, ran under the porch, and the dog ran after him.

Table 2.9. Sentence Structure and Clauses

Sentence Structure	Independent Clauses	Dependent Clauses
Simple	1	0
Compound	2 +	0
Complex	1	1 +
Compound-complex	2 +	1 +

12. Which of the following is a compound sentence?

A) The turtle swam slowly around the pond.

B) Alligators generally lie still, but they can move with lightning speed.

C) Mice are most likely to come out at night after other animals have gone to sleep.

D) Squirrels, to prepare for winter, gather and hide seeds and nuts underground.

PUNCTUATION

Terminal punctuation marks are used to end sentences. The **PERIOD** (.) ends declarative (statement) and imperative (command) sentences. The **QUESTION MARK** (?) terminates interrogative sentences (questions). Lastly, **EXCLAMATION POINTS** end exclamatory sentences, in which the writer or speaker is exhibiting intense emotion or energy.

> Sarah and I are attending a concert.
> How many people are attending the concert?
> What a great show that was!

The colon and the semicolon, though often confused, each have a unique set of rules for their use. While both punctuation marks are used to join clauses, the construction of the clauses and the relationship between them is different. The **SEMICOLON** (;) is used to join two independent clauses (IC; IC) that are closely related.

> I need to buy a new car soon; my old car broke down last month.

The **COLON** (:) is used to introduce a list, definition, or clarification. The clause preceding the colon has to be independent, but what follows the colon can be an independent clause, a dependent clause, or a phrase.

> The buffet offers three choices: ham, turkey, or roast beef.
> He decided to drive instead of taking the train: he didn't think the train would arrive in time.

COMMAS show pauses in the text or set information apart from the main text. There are lots of rules for comma usage, so only the most common are summarized below.

1. Commas separate two independent clauses along with a coordinating conjunction.
   George ordered the steak, <u>but</u> Bruce preferred the ham.

2. Commas separate coordinate adjectives.
   She made herself a big bowl of <u>cold, delicious</u> ice cream.

3. Commas separate items in a series.
   The list of groceries included <u>cream, coffee, donuts, and tea.</u>

4. Commas separate introductory words and phrases from the rest of the sentence.
   <u>For example</u>, we have thirty students who demand a change.

5. Commas set off non-essential information and appositives.
   Estelle, <u>our newly elected chairperson</u>, will be in attendance.

6. Commas set off the day and month of a date within a text.
   I was born on February <u>16, 1988</u>.

7. Commas set up numbers in a text of more than four digits.
   We expect <u>25,000</u> visitors to the new museum.

8. Commas set off the names of cities from their states, territories, or provinces.
   She lives in <u>Houston, Texas</u>.

QUOTATION MARKS have a number of different purposes. They enclose titles of short, or relatively short, literary works such as short stories, chapters, and poems. (The titles of longer works, like novels and anthologies, are italicized.) Additionally, quotation marks are used to enclose direct quotations within the text of a document where the quotation is integrated into the text. Writers also use quotation marks to set off dialogue.

> We will be reading the poem "Bright Star" in class today.
> The poem opens with the line "Bright star, would I were steadfast
> as thou art."

APOSTROPHES, sometimes referred to as single quotation marks, have several different purposes.

1. They show possession.
   boy's watch, Ronald and Maria's house

2. They replace missing letters, numerals, and signs.
   do not = don't, 1989 = '89

3. They form plurals of letters, numerals, and signs.
   A's, 10's

Less commonly used punctuation marks include:

▶ EN DASH (–): indicates a range

▶ EM DASH (—): shows an abrupt break in a sentence and emphasizes the words within the em dashes

▶ PARENTHESES ( ): enclose nonessential information

▶ BRACKETS [ ]: enclose added words to a quotation and add insignificant information within parentheses

▶ SLASH (/): separates lines of poetry within a text or indicates interchangeable terminology

▶ ELLIPSES (…): indicates that information has been removed from a quotation or creates a reflective pause

13. Which sentence includes an improperly placed comma?

    A) Ella, Cassie, and Cameron drove to South Carolina together.

    B) Trying to impress his friends, Carl ended up totaling his car.

    C) Ice cream is my favorite food, it is so cold and creamy.

    D) Mowing the lawn, Navid discovered a family of baby rabbits.

14. The following sentence contains an error. How should it be rewritten?

Oak trees—with proper care—can grow taller than thirty feet; providing shade for people, shelter for animals, and perches for birds.

    A) replace the em dashes with commas

    B) remove the comma after *people*

    C) insert an apostrophe at the end of *animals*

    D) replace the semicolon with a comma

Capitalization

CAPITALIZATION is writing the first letter of a word in uppercase and the remaining letters in lowercase. Capitalization is used in three main contexts. The first, and most common, is in the first word after a period or the first word of a text. For example, the first word in each sentence of this paragraph is capitalized.

The second most common usage of capitalization is for proper nouns or adjectives derived from proper nouns. For instance, **F**rance—as the name of a country—is capitalized. Similarly, **F**rench, the adjective derived from the proper noun *France*, is also capitalized. There is an exception to this rule: when the adjective has taken on a meaning independent of the original proper noun. For example, the term *french fries* is not capitalized.

The third usage of capitalization is in a title or honorific that appears before a name: "**P**resident George Washington never lived in the capital." If, however, that same title is used *instead of* the name, or if the name and title are separated by a comma, it remains lowercase. For example, "The first **p**resident, George Washington, never lived in the capital" or "The **p**resident did not originally live in the capital."

EXAMPLE

15. Which sentence CORRECTLY uses capitalization?

    A) Robert and Kelly raced across the River in their small boats.

    B) ducks flying in a V-formation cross the Midwest in the fall.

    C) The chairwoman of the board, Keisha Johnson, will lead today's meeting.

    D) The Senators from Virginia and Louisiana strongly favor the bill.

Common Language Errors
SUBJECT-VERB AGREEMENT

Verbs must agree in number with their subjects. Common rules for subject/verb agreement are given below.

1. Single subjects agree with single verbs; plural subjects agree with plural verbs.
   The <u>girl walks</u> her dog.
   The <u>girls walk</u> their dogs.

2. Ignore words between the subject and the verb: agreement must exist between the subject and verb.
   The new <u>library</u> ~~with its many books and rooms~~ <u>fills</u> a long-felt need.

3. Compound subjects joined by *and* typically take a plural verb unless considered one item.
   <u>Correctness and precision are required</u> for all good writing.
   <u>Macaroni and cheese makes</u> a great snack for children.

4. The linking verbs agree with the subject and not the subject complement (predicate nominative).
   My <u>favorite</u> is strawberries and apples.
   My <u>favorites are</u> strawberries and apples.

5. When a relative pronoun (*who, whom, which, that*) is used as the subject of the clause, the verb will agree with the antecedent of the relative pronoun.
   This is the <u>student who is receiving</u> an award.
   These are the <u>students who are receiving</u> awards.

6. All single, indefinite pronouns agree with single verbs.
   <u>Neither</u> of the students <u>is</u> happy about the play.
   <u>Each</u> of the many cars <u>is</u> on the grass.
   Every <u>one</u> of the administrators <u>speaks</u> highly of Trevor.

EXAMPLE

16. Which sentence in the following list is CORRECT in its subject and verb agreement?
    A) My sister and my best friend lives in Chicago.
    B) My parents or my brother is going to pick me up from the airport.
    C) Neither of the students refuse to take the exam.
    D) The team were playing a great game until the rain started.

PRONOUN-ANTECEDENT AGREEMENT

Similarly, pronouns must agree with their antecedents (the words they replaced) in number; however, some pronouns also require gender agreement (*him, her*). PRONOUN/ ANTECEDENT AGREEMENT rules can be found below:

1. Antecedents joined by *and* typically require a plural pronoun.
    The <u>children and their dogs</u> enjoyed <u>their</u> day at the beach.
    If the two nouns refer to the same person, a singular pronoun is preferable.
    My <u>best friend and confidant</u> still lives in <u>her</u> log cabin.

2. For compound antecedents joined by *or*, the pronoun agrees with the nearer or nearest antecedent.
    Either the resident mice <u>or the manager's cat</u> gets <u>itself</u> a meal of good leftovers.

3. When indefinite pronouns function in a sentence, the pronoun must agree with the number of the indefinite pronoun.
    <u>Neither</u> student finished <u>his or her</u> assignment.
    <u>Both</u> students finished <u>their</u> assignments.

4. When collective nouns function as antecedents, the pronoun choice will be singular or plural depending on the function of the collective.
    The <u>audience</u> was cheering as <u>it</u> rose to <u>its</u> feet in unison.
    Our <u>family</u> are spending <u>their</u> vacations in Maine, Hawaii, and Rome.

5. When *each* and *every* precede the antecedent, the pronoun agreement will be singular.
    <u>Each and every man, woman, and child</u> brings unique qualities to <u>his or her</u> family.
    <u>Every creative writer, technical writer, and research writer</u> is attending <u>his or her</u> assigned lecture.

How would you complete the following sentence? "Every boy and girl should check _____ homework before turning it in." Many people would use the pronoun *their*. But since the antecedent is "every boy and girl," technically, the correct answer would be *his* or *her*. Using *they* or *their* in similar situations is increasingly accepted in formal speech, however. It is unlikely that you will see questions like this appear on the GED, but if you do, it is safest to use the technically correct response.

EXAMPLE

17. Which sentence in the following list is CORRECT in its pronoun and antecedent agreement?

    A) The grandchildren and their cousins enjoyed their day at the park.

    B) Most of the grass has lost their deep color.

    C) The jury was relieved as their commitment came to a close.

    D) Every boy and girl must learn to behave themselves in school.

48   Accepted, Inc. | **GED Reasoning Through Language Arts Study Guide**

18. Which sentence in the following list is CORRECT in its pronoun and antecedent agreement?

    A)   Either my brother or my dad will bring their van to pick us up.

    B)   The university is having their tenth fundraiser tonight.

    C)   Alyssa and Jacqueline bought herself a big lunch today.

    D)   Each dog, cat, and rabbit has its own bowl and blanket.

VERB-TENSE AGREEMENT

In any passage, verb tense should be consistent and make sense in context of other verbs, adverbs, and general meaning. Verb tense questions appear frequently on the GED, so pay attention to the context of the entire passage.

> **INCORRECT:** Deborah <u>was speaking</u> with her colleague when her boss <u>will appear</u>, demanding a meeting.

In this sentence, the subject, *Deborah*, is acting in an ongoing event in the past, so the verb describing this action, *speaking*, is conjugated in the continuous past tense. In the context of the sentence, the appearance of her boss is a completed event that happens during the conversation. The verb describing the boss' appearance should be conjugated in the simple past tense. The corrected sentence reads as follows:

> **CORRECT:** Deborah <u>was speaking</u> with her colleague when her boss <u>appeared</u>, demanding a meeting.

One clue to the correct conjugation of the verb *appeared* is the adverb *when*, which implies that a completed event occurred to interrupt the ongoing event (in this case, Deborah's talk with her colleague).

Pay attention to how verbs are conjugated in the beginning of a sentence or passage, and look for clues to spot any errors in verb tense agreement.

EXAMPLE

19. The following sentence contains an error. How should it be rewritten?

Veronica attended cooking classes, and she goes to yoga classes too.

    A)   Veronica attends cooking classes, and she went to yoga classes too.

    B)   Veronica attended cooking classes, and she went to yoga classes too.

    C)   Veronica attended cooking classes; she goes to yoga classes too.

    D)   Veronica attended cooking classes. She goes to yoga classes too.

PARALLELISM

Errors in **PARALLELISM** prevent a writer from creating a smooth flow, or coherence, from word to word and sentence to sentence. Writers should create parallel structure in words, phrases, and clauses wherever two or more similar and equally important ideas exist next to each other in a sentence. Errors in parallel structure frequently appear in sentences with verb phrases, prepositional phrases, and correlative conjunctions like *either…or, neither…nor,* and *not only…but also.*

> **INCORRECT:** Adia could <u>program</u> computers, <u>repair</u> cars, and <u>knew how to make</u> croissants.
>
> **CORRECT:** Adia could <u>program</u> computers, <u>repair</u> cars, and <u>bake</u> croissants.

In the corrected sentence, the verbs are aligned in parallel structure. Furthermore, the first sentence contains a verb error. By omitting "program computers, repair cars," the sentence reads "Adia could…knew how to make croissants" Rewriting the sentence in parallel structure corrects the verb error.

In sentences with multiple prepositional phrases in a parallel series, the preposition must be repeated unless the same preposition begins each phrase.

> **INCORRECT:** You can park your car <u>in</u> the garage, the carport, or <u>on</u> the street.
>
> **CORRECT:** You can park your car <u>in</u> the garage, <u>in</u> the carport, or <u>on</u> the street.

EXAMPLE

20. The following sentence contains an error. How should it be rewritten?

    Shelly achieved more at nursing school because she was going to bed earlier, eating healthy food, and she started to stay home and study more.

    A) Shelly achieved more at nursing school. She was going to bed earlier, eating healthy food, and she started to stay home and study more.

    B) Shelly achieved more at nursing school because she was going to bed earlier, eating healthy food, and studying more.

    C) Shelly achieved more at nursing school; she was going to bed earlier, eating healthy food, and she started to stay home and study more.

    D) Shelly achieved more at nursing school; she was going to bed earlier, and she started to eat healthy food and studying more.

SENTENCE CONSTRUCTION ERRORS

SENTENCE ERRORS fall into three categories: fragments, comma splices (comma fault), and fused sentences (run-on). A **FRAGMENT** occurs when a group of words is not a complete sentence but is punctuated like one. The fragment might be a phrase or a dependent clause. To fix a fragment, an independent clause needs to be created.

> FRAGMENT (PHRASE): The girl in my class who asks a lot of questions.
> CORRECT: The girl in my class who asks a lot of questions sits in the back row.
> FRAGMENT (DEPENDENT CLAUSE): Because of the big storm we had last weekend.
> CORRECT: Because of the big storm we had last weekend,
> the park will be closed.

A COMMA SPLICE (comma fault) occurs when two independent clauses are joined together in a paragraph with only a comma to "splice" them together. FUSED (run-on) sentences occur when two independent clauses are joined with no punctuation whatsoever. To fix a comma splice or fused sentence, add the correct punctuation and/or conjunction.

> COMMA SPLICE: My family eats turkey at Thanksgiving, we
> eat ham at Christmas.
> CORRECT: My family eats turkey at Thanksgiving, and we
> eat ham at Christmas.
> CORRECT: My family eats turkey at Thanksgiving. We eat ham at Christmas.
> CORRECT: My family eats turkey at Thanksgiving; we eat ham at Christmas.
> FUSED SENTENCE: I bought a chocolate pie from the bakery it was delicious.
> CORRECT: I bought a chocolate pie from the bakery. It was delicious.
> CORRECT: I bought a chocolate pie from the bakery, and it was delicious.
> CORRECT: I bought a chocolate pie from the bakery; it was delicious.

EXAMPLE

21. Which of the following is CORRECTLY punctuated?
    A) Since she went to the store.
    B) The football game ended in a tie, the underdog caught up in the fourth quarter.
    C) The mall is closing early today so we'll have to go shopping tomorrow.
    D) When the players dropped their gloves, a fight broke out on the ice hockey rink floor.

EASILY CONFUSED WORDS

A, AN: *a* precedes words beginning with consonants or consonant sounds; *an* precedes words beginning with vowels or vowel sounds.

AFFECT, EFFECT: *affect* is most often a verb; *effect* is usually a noun. (*The experience affected me significantly* OR *The experience had a significant effect on me.*)

AMONG, AMONGST, BETWEEN: *among* is used for a group of more than two people or items; *amongst* is an uncommon, archaic term; *between* distinguishes two people or items.

AMOUNT, NUMBER: *amount* is used for noncountable sums; *number* is used with countable nouns.

CITE, SITE: the verb *cite* credits an author of a quotation, paraphrase, or summary; the noun *site* is a location.

EVERY DAY, EVERYDAY: *every day* is an indefinite adjective modifying a noun; *everyday* is a one-word adjective implying frequent occurrence. (*Our visit to the Minnesota State Fair is an everyday activity during August.*)

FEWER, LESS: *fewer* is used with a countable noun; *less* is used with a noncountable noun. (*Fewer parents are experiencing stress since the new teacher was hired; parents are experiencing less stress since the new teacher was hired.*)

GOOD, WELL: good is always the adjective; *well* is always the adverb except in cases of health. (*He writes well. She felt well after the surgery.*)

IMPLIED, INFERRED: *implied* is something a speaker does; *inferred* is something the listener does after assessing the speaker's message. (*The speaker implied something mysterious, but I inferred the wrong thing.*)

IRREGARDLESS, REGARDLESS: *irregardless* is nonstandard usage and should be avoided; *regardless* is the proper usage of the transitional statement.

ITS, IT'S: *its* is a possessive pronoun; *it's* is a contraction for *it is*.

PRINCIPAL, PRINCIPLE: as a noun, *principal* is an authority figure, often the head of a school; as an adjective, *principal* means *main*; the noun *principle* means idea or belief. (*The principal of the school spoke on the principal meaning of the main principles of the school.*)

QUOTE, QUOTATION: *quote* is a verb; *quotation* is a noun.

SHOULD OF, SHOULD HAVE: *should of* is improper usage—*of* is not a helping verb and therefore cannot complete the verb phrase; *should have* is the proper usage. (*He should have driven.*)

THAN, THEN: *than* sets up a comparison; *then* indicates a reference to a point in time. (*When I said that I liked the hat better than the gloves, my sister laughed; then she bought both for me.*)

THEIR, THERE, THEY'RE: *their* is the possessive case of the pronoun *they*. *There* is the demonstrative pronoun indicating location or place. *They're* is a contraction of the words *they are*.

TO LIE (TO RECLINE), TO LAY (TO PLACE): *to lie* is the intransitive verb meaning *to recline*; *to lay* is the transitive verb meaning *to place something*. (*I lie out in the sun; I lay my towel on the beach.*)

WHO, WHOM: *who* is the subject relative pronoun. (*My son, who is a good student, studies hard.*) Here, the son is carrying out the action of studying, so the pronoun is a subject pronoun (*who*). *Whom* is the object relative pronoun. (*My son, whom the other students admire, studies hard.*) Here, *son* is the object of the other students' admiration, so the pronoun standing in for him, *whom*, is an object pronoun.

YOUR, YOU'RE: *your* is the possessive case of the pronoun *you*. *You're* is a contraction of the words *you are*.

EXAMPLE

22. Which of the following sentences contains an error?

    A)   I invited fewer people to my birthday party this year.

    B)   The students asked the principle to postpone the meeting.

    C)   My sister baked cookies then asked me to help clean the kitchen.

    D)   She paints well even though she has no formal training.

Test Your Knowledge

Select the underlined portion of the sentence that contains a grammatical error. If the sentence is correct, choose (D) No error.

1. Ukrainians **(A)**celebrate a holiday called Malanka during which men **(B)**dress in costumes and **(C)**plays tricks on their neighbors. **(D)**No error

2. Because of **(A)**its distance from the sun, the planet Neptune **(B)**has seasons that last the **(C)**equivalent of forty-one Earth years. **(D)**No error

3. In addition to the disastrous effects an active volcano can have on **(A)** it's immediate surroundings, an eruption can also pose a threat to passing aircraft and **(B)**can temporarily change the temperature of **(C)**Earth's atmosphere. **(D)**No error

4. The employer **(A)**decided that, **(B)**due to the high cost of health care, he could not afford to offer **(C)**no other benefits to his employees. **(D)**No error

5. Though Puerto Rico is known popularly for **(A)**its beaches, its landscape also **(B)**includes mountains, which are home to many of the **(C)**island's rural villages. **(D)**No error

6. The photographer **(A)**, specializes in shooting portraits and taking still lifes, but she also **(B)**likes to accept more challenging assignments, such as **(C)** photographing wildlife. **(D)**No error

7. In the fight **(A)**against obesity, **(B)**countries' around the world are imposing taxes on sodas and other sugary drinks **(C)**in hopes of curbing unhealthy habits. **(D)**No error

8. The **(A)**Black Death, often thought of as a concern of times past, **(B)** continued to spread among rodent populations even today, occasionally making **(C)**its way into a human host. **(D)**No error

9. The storm chasers, who **(A)**stressed and emphasized the importance of caution in their work, **(B)**decided not to go out when the sheets of rain made visibility **(C)**too low. **(D)**No error

10. James **(A)**having already been awake for nineteen hours, after a **(B)**twelve-hour work day, when he **(C)**received the news. **(D)**No error

Select the answer choice that best completes the sentence.

11. The famously high death toll at the end of the Civil War was not due only to battle losses; _____ large numbers of soldiers and civilians fell ill and died as a result of living conditions during the war.

    A) in addition,

    B) therefore,

    C) however,

    D) on the other hand,

12. The public defense attorney was able to maintain her optimism despite _____.

    A) her dearth of courtroom wins, lack of free time she had, and growing list of clients she was helping.

    B) her dearth of courtroom wins, lack of free time, and growing list of clients.

    C) her dearth of courtroom wins, the free time she lacked, and the list of clients she was growing.

    D) the losses she had experienced, the free time she lacked, and her growing client list.

13. _____ the stethoscope underwent a number of reiterations before the modern form of the instrument was introduced in the 1850s.

    A) Being invented in France in the early nineteenth century,

    B) It was invented in France in the early nineteenth century,

    C) Though it was invented in France in the nineteenth century,

    D) Invented in France in the early nineteenth century,

14. In 1983, almost twenty years after his death, T. S. Eliot won two Tony Awards for his contributions to the well-loved musical *Cats,* _____

    A) it was based on a book of his poetry.

    B) which was based on a book of his poetry.

    C) being based on a book of his poetry.

    D) having been based on a book of his poetry.

15. Typically, water _____ before falling to Earth again as precipitation.

    A) remain in the sky in cloud form for fewer than ten days

    B) remain in the sky in cloud form for fewer then ten days

    C) remains in the sky in cloud form for fewer than ten days

    D) will remain in the sky in cloud form for fewer then ten days

16. Parrots, among the most intelligent birds in the world, have been prized pets for many _____

    A) centuries, in fact, the first recorded instance of parrot training was written in the thirteenth century.

    B) centuries, but the first recorded instance of parrot training was written in the thirteenth century.

    C) centuries, writing the first recorded instance of parrot training in the thirteenth century.

    D) centuries; in fact, the first recorded instance of parrot training was written in the thirteenth century.

17. _____ research into automating vehicle processes began as early as the 1920s.

    A) Before self-driving vehicles are just now being introduced on the automotive market,

    B) Though self-driving vehicles are just now being introduced on the automotive market,

    C) Because self-driving vehicles are just now being introduced on the automotive market,

    D) Self-driving vehicles are just now being introduced on the automotive market,

18. The exotic pet _____ is a significant concern for environmentalists and animal rights advocates around the world.

    A) trade, which involves both the capturing of wild animals and the captive breeding of wild species,

    B) trade, which involves both the capturing of wild animals and they breed wild species in captivity,

    C) trade involves both the capturing of wild animals and the captive breeding of wild species, it

    D) trade, it involves both the capturing of wild animals and the captive breeding of wild species,

19. Hurricanes, _____ have been the cause of almost two million deaths in the last two hundred years.

    A) which costs the United States roughly $5 billion per year in damages,

    B) having cost the United States roughly $5 billion per year in damages,

    C) which cost the United States roughly $5 billion per year in damages,

    D) have cost the United States roughly $5 billion per year in damages,

20. In 1903, Pennsylvania _____ in response, however, artists like Walt McDougall began depicting politicians in an even less flattering light—as inanimate objects such as trees and mugs.

    A) depicting politicians as animals, passed a law prohibiting cartoonists in order to curb criticism by the press;

    B) prohibiting cartoonists from depicting politicians as animals, passed a law in order to curb criticism by the press;

    C) passed a law prohibiting cartoonists from depicting politicians in order to curb criticism as animals by the press;

    D) passed a law prohibiting cartoonists from depicting politicians as animals in order to curb criticism by the press;

Select the answer choice that best completes the sentence in the passage.

Anyone who has been given a nickname knows that these informal labels can sometimes be difficult to shake. In the 1980s, one group of young actors earned a group nickname—the Brat Pack—that would follow them for decades. While some members of the Brat Pack still went on to have successful **(21)**_____ struggled to make their own names stand out against the backdrop of the group.

The members of the Brat Pack earned their fame by appearing together in a series of films made for teen and young adult audiences. **(22)**_____ one of these movies was made in the early 1980s, the Brat Pack label did not appear until 1985, when *New York Magazine* writer David Blum wrote an article about his experience socializing with some of the group members. The article **(23)**_____ these young actors as immature, unprofessional, and spoiled, and though Blum's experience with them was limited to one night with just three individuals, his label quickly caught on and tarnished the reputations of many of the other young actors who worked alongside the three. Many of these individuals struggled professionally as a result of the negative label, and most of them denied being a part of any such group.

Today, despite the initial repercussions of the unfortunate nickname, the Brat Pack label is still in use, largely because of the **(24)**_____ relevance and significance of the Brat Pack films. Most of these films are coming-of-age stories, in which one or more of the characters gains experience or learns an important lesson about adult life. For example, in the most famous of these films, *The Breakfast Club*, the five main characters, **(25)**_____ are all from different social circles at one high school, learn to look past labels and appearances and find that they have more in common than they ever imagined.

Because of the talent and the relatability of the Brat Pack members, these characters and their stories continue to appeal to young people and influence popular culture in the new millennium. Thus, the Brat Pack nickname has been freed of its negative connotations by the actors who once despised and wore the label.

21.
- **A)** careers; others
- **B)** careers, others
- **C)** careers, but others
- **D)** careers. Others

22.
- **A)** Though the first
- **B)** The first
- **C)** Because the first
- **D)** Consequently, the first

23.
- **A)** is portraying
- **B)** would portray
- **C)** was portraying
- **D)** portrayed

24.
- **A)** ongoing and perpetual
- **B)** perpetually ongoing
- **C)** never-ending, perpetual
- **D)** ongoing

25.
- **A)** whom
- **B)** who
- **C)** which
- **D)** and

Answer Key
EXAMPLES

1. **B) is correct.** Nouns are people, places, things, or ideas; they usually act as the subject or object in a sentence.

2. **D) is correct.** The reflexive pronoun *ourselves* refers back to the subject of the sentence. Because it is in the first person plural, the subject should also be in the first person plural (*we*).

3. **A) is correct.** The phrase *by this time tomorrow* describes as action that will take place and be completed in the future, so the future perfect tense (*will have arrived*) should be used.

4. **C) is correct.** *Package* is the direct object of the verb *brought*.

5. **B) is correct.** The speaker is comparing today's run to the norm, not to any additional instances, so the comparative is acceptable here. Furthermore, the word *than* appears, a clue that the comparative is appropriate. *Less* is the irregular comparative form of *little*.

6. **D) is correct.** *Carelessly* is an adverb modifying *sped* and explaining *how* the driving occurred. The subject was not mindful as he drove; he raced through a yellow light when he should have exercised caution.

7. **A) is correct.** This sentence includes two independent clauses: "He liked to cook" and "baking was his specialty." They can be connected with a comma and coordinating conjunction (the conjunction *and* is appropriate here). The sentence could also be written with a semicolon and no conjunction.

8. **A) is correct.** "While they read the paper" is a dependent clause; the subordinating conjunction *while* connects it to the independent clause "Anne and Peter drank their coffee languidly."

9. **B) is correct.** "Through the tunnel" is a prepositional phrase explaining the relationship between the subjects and the tunnel using the preposition *through* and the object *the tunnel*.

10. **D) is correct.** *Yay* is an expression of emotion and has no other grammatical purpose in the sentence.

11. **D) is correct.** The phrase is a verbal phrase modifying the noun *Rachel*. It begins with the word *dodging*, derived from the verb to *dodge*.

12. **B) is correct.** "Alligators...still" and "they...speed" are two independent clauses connected by a comma and the coordinating conjunction *but*.

13. **C) is correct.** "Ice cream... food" and "it...creamy" are two independent clauses. The writer should include a coordinating conjunction like *for* or separate the clauses with a semicolon.

14. **D) is correct.** "Providing shade..." is not an independent clause; therefore it cannot be preceded by a semicolon.

15. **C) is correct.** *Keisha Johnson,* as a proper noun, should be capitalized, but "chairwoman of the board" should not be because it is separated from the name by a comma.

16. **B) is correct.** The verb agrees with the closest subject—in this case, the singular *brother*.

17. **A) is correct.** The plural antecedents *grandchildren* and *cousins* match the plural possessive pronoun *their*.

18. **D) is correct.** When *each* precedes the antecedent, the pronoun agreement is singular. The pronoun *its* therefore agrees with the antecedents *Each dog, cat, and rabbit*.

19. **B) is correct.** In this sentence, the verbs *attended* and *went* are both correctly conjugated in the simple past tense.

20. **B) is correct.** In this sentence, three related clauses are written in parallel structure using the participles *going, eating,* and *studying*.

21. **D) is correct.** This is a complete sentence that is punctuated properly with a comma between the dependent and independent clauses.

22. **B) is correct.** A principle is a belief; a principal is the head of a school.

TEST YOUR KNOWLEDGE

1. **C) is correct.** *Plays* is a singular verb and does not correctly pair with the plural subject *men*; *men dress* and *play*.

2. **D) is correct.** No errors are present in this sentence.

3. **A) is correct.** *It's* is a contraction of the phrase *it is*; this context requires the possessive form (*its surroundings*).

4. **C) is correct.** Because it is a negative, *no other* inaccurately discounts the first negative (*not*) and creates a double negative (*could not afford no other*); it should be changed to *any other*.

5. **D) is correct.** No error exists in this sentence.

6. **A) is correct.** A comma should not be included in this location, as it separates the subject (*photographer*) and the verb (*specializes*).

7. **B) is correct.** *Countries'* is a plural possessive but should be acting as a plural subject; the correct format of the word is *countries* (*around the world*).

8. **B) is correct.** *Continued* is a past-tense verb; however, it should be present tense (*continues*) in order to align with the time mentioned later in the sentence (*even today*).

9. **A) is correct.** *Stressed and emphasized* have similar definitions in this context; only one word needs to be used.

10. **A) is correct.** *Having*, a participle, turns this sentence into a fragment by removing the verb; to improve the sentence, *having* should be replaced with *had*.

11. **A) is correct.** *In addition* is the appropriate introductory phrase to signify the additive relationship between the two clauses.

12. **B) is correct.** In this iteration, all items in the list are nouns (*dearth*, *lack*, and *list*), followed by prepositions (*of*) and objects of the prepositions (*wins*, *time*, and *clients*).

13. **D) is correct.** *Invented*, the past participle of *invent*, appropriately introduces this participial phrase that provides more information about the subject of the sentence (*stethoscope*).

14. **B) is correct.** *Which* is used correctly here to introduce an additional, nonrestrictive clause about an element of the sentence (*the musical*).

15. **C) is correct.** *Remains* is a singular, present-tense verb that agrees with its subject *water*, which is noncountable and therefore singular; *than* is a conjunction used correctly here to express inequality between two things (amount of time the water is in the sky and ten days).

16. **D) is correct.** The semicolon is used appropriately here to join two independent, related clauses; *in fact* signifies an interesting detail to follow.

17. **B) is correct.** *Though* is used correctly in this sentence to show a slight contradiction between the assumption (that self-driving cars are new) and the truth (that vehicle automation has been a topic of study for many decades).

18. **A) is correct.** The appositive phrase is correctly enclosed with commas; the items inside the commas are parallel (*the capturing of wild animals and the captive breeding of wild species*).

19. **C) is correct.** *Which cost* is a clear, concise way to set off the nonrestrictive appositive phrase.

20. **D) is correct.** Modifying relationships are clear: *Pennsylvania* is followed by its verb *passed* and the description of the law (*prohibiting cartoonists from*...) immediately follows the word *law*; the reason for the law (*in order to*...) comes after the description of the law.

21. **B) is correct.** The comma following *careers* correctly separates the independent clause from the following dependent clause.

22. **A) is correct.** The subordinating conjunction *though* correctly begins the sentence; it creates a relationship that makes good sense between the opening subordinate clause and the independent clause that follows.

23. **D) is correct.** The past-tense verb *portrayed* agrees with the past-tense verbs *was* and *caught* that appear later in the sentence.

24. **D) is correct.** Since the two adjectives are synonyms, using just one of them is sufficient. Using both would be redundant.

25. **B) is correct.** The subject form of the relative pronoun *who* correctly appears here. The word functions as a subject, not an object.

CHAPTER THREE
The Essay

The GED requires an essay in the Reasoning Through Language Arts section. You will be provided with a prompt and asked to take a position on it. To do well on the essay, take a clear side on the issue put forth in the prompt. Support your perspective with strong arguments and specific examples. An effective essay is clearly organized and structured, displays strong vocabulary, and features complex sentences.

There are two common types of essays:

▶ an expository essay explains an issue without taking sides or promoting a perspective

▶ a persuasive essay argues in favor of or against an issue or perspective

For the GED, you'll be writing a persuasive essay.

Writing a Thesis Statement

A **THESIS STATEMENT** articulates the main argument of the essay. No essay is complete without it: the structure and organization of the essay revolves around the thesis statement. The thesis statement is simply the writer's main idea or argument. It usually appears at the end of the introduction.

In a good thesis statement, the author states his or her idea or argument and why it is correct or true.

EXAMPLE

Take a position on the following topic in your essay. You can choose to write about either of the two viewpoints discussed in the prompt, or you may argue for a third point of view.

Many scientists argue that recent unusual weather patterns, such as powerful hurricanes and droughts, are due to climate change triggered by human activity. They argue that automobiles, oil and gas production, and manufacturing generate carbon emissions that artificially heat the atmosphere, resulting in extreme weather patterns. Others disagree. Some researchers and media pundits argue that climate change is natural, and that extreme weather has always been a feature of Earth's atmosphere.

Around the world more people than ever before are driving cars, and industrial production is at an all-time high: it is obvious that human activity is affecting the atmosphere and causing extreme weather events.

I believe that temperatures and storms are more extreme than ever because of the environmental impact of human activity; not only do scientists have overwhelming evidence that climate change is unnatural, but I can also personally remember when there were fewer storms and variations in temperature.

Society needs cars and manufacturing, but governments should restrict harmful emissions released into the atmosphere so we can slow down climate change and save lives.

Structuring the Essay

On the GED, a strong essay will have an introduction, a body, and a conclusion. While there are many ways to organize an essay, on this exam it is most important that the essay is clearly structured. There is no need to get too complicated: this simple structure will do.

INTRODUCTIONS

DID YOU KNOW?

If you're not sure what to include in your introduction, start your essay with just the thesis statement. You can go back and complete the introduction once the rest of the essay is finished.

Some writers struggle with the introduction, but it is actually an opportunity to present your idea or argument. On the GED, the introduction can be one paragraph that ends with the thesis statement. In the rest of the paragraph, the writer provides some context for his or her argument. This context might include counterarguments, a preview of specific examples to be discussed later on, acknowledgement of the complexities of the issue, or even a reference to personal experience. The writer can reexamine some of these issues in the conclusion.

EXAMPLE

In the example below, the writer has written an introduction that includes context for her argument: background information, a counterargument, and personal experience. As a result, the reader has a better idea of how complex the issue is and why the writer feels the way she does. The thesis statement appears at the end of the paragraph; as a result of the introduction as a whole, the thesis statement has more impact.

A century ago, there were barely any cars on the road. Oil had just been discovered in a few parts of the world. Industrial production existed but had not yet exploded with the introduction of the assembly line. Refineries and factories were not yet churning out the chemical emissions they are today. Certainly, hurricanes and droughts occurred, but the populations and infrastructure affected were far smaller. Now, scientists have evidence that human activity—like pollution from industry and cars—is affecting the atmosphere and making weather more extreme. In 2017, millions of people were affected by hurricanes and wildfires. It is true that some researchers disagree that human activity has caused these and other extreme weather events. But why take the risk? If we can limit destruction now and in the future, we should. Extreme weather events are a danger to people all around the world. Society needs cars and manufacturing, but governments should restrict harmful emissions released into the atmosphere so we can slow down climate change and save lives.

THE BODY PARAGRAPHS

Most writers find the body of the essay the easiest part to write. The body of the essay is simply several paragraphs, each beginning with a topic sentence. Each paragraph usually addresses an example that supports the argument made in the thesis statement or, in the case of an expository essay, explains the writer's reasoning. On the GED, you may use specific examples or personal anecdotes, present problems and solutions, or compare and contrast ideas. You do not need to refer to any outside literature or documentation.

To strengthen the body of the essay, writers will maintain consistency in paragraphs, always beginning with a topic sentence, which introduces the main idea of each paragraph. Each paragraph deals with its own main topic, but writers should use transition words and phrases to link paragraphs with each other. A good essay maintains readability and flow.

EXAMPLE

This example body paragraph is related to the introduction provided above. It provides reasoning and historical evidence for the author's argument that human activity is impacting the earth and causing climate change.

Human industrial activity has been growing exponentially, putting more pollution into the atmosphere than ever. Over the past forty years, large countries like China and India have become industrialized and manufacture many of the world's products. As their populations become more prosperous, demand for automobiles also rises, putting more cars on the road—and exhaust in the air. While industrial development has benefited Asia and other areas, carbon emissions that cause climate change have multiplied. Meanwhile, previously industrialized countries in Europe and North America continue to produce carbon emissions. In the nineteenth century, only a few countries had industrial sectors; today, global industry strains the environment like never before. The past 150 years have seen unprecedented industrial growth. Even if the climate changes naturally over time, it cannot be denied that recent human activity has suddenly generated enormous amounts of carbon emissions that have impacted the atmosphere. Scientists say that the earth is warming as a result.

CONCLUSIONS

The conclusion does not need to be long. Its purpose is to wrap up the essay, reminding the reader why the topic and the writer's argument is important. It is an opportunity for the writer to reexamine the thesis statement and ideas in the introduction. It is a time to reinforce the argument, not just to repeat the introduction.

EXAMPLE

This example is taken from the same essay as the introduction and body paragraph above. It reinforces the writer's argument without simply repeating what she said in the introduction. The writer does address the topics she spoke about in the introduction (climate change and protecting people from extreme weather) but she does not simply rewrite the thesis: she calls for action.

No doubt, scientists, pundits, and politicians will continue to argue over the reasons for extreme weather. Meanwhile, Mother Nature will continue to wreak havoc on vulnerable areas regardless of what we think. Because we have proof that climate change is related to extreme weather and we know that extreme weather threatens people's lives, the time to act is now. We can take steps to mitigate pollution without lowering quality of life. Doing anything else is irresponsible—and for some, deadly.

Providing Supporting Evidence

As discussed above, a good essay should have specific evidence or examples that support the thesis statement. On the GED, a specific example should be something related to the idea of the paragraph and the essay, not a new idea. A specific example can be from your general knowledge; you do not need to know about specific academic issues to do well on the essay. Remember, you are being tested on your reasoning and argumentative skills.

The following are some examples of general statements and specific statements that provide more detailed support:

GENERAL: Human industrial activity has been growing exponentially, putting more pollution into the atmosphere than ever.

SPECIFIC: Over the past forty years, large countries like China and India have become industrialized and manufacture many of the world's products. As their populations become more prosperous, demand for automobiles also rises, putting more cars on the road—and exhaust in the air.

SPECIFIC: Meanwhile, previously industrialized countries in Europe and North America continue to produce carbon emissions. In the nineteenth century, only a few countries had industrial sectors; today, global industry strains the environment like never before.

GENERAL: More people than ever are affected by extreme weather.

SPECIFIC: In 2017, several hurricanes affected the United States and the Caribbean. In Texas, Hurricane Harvey led to historic flooding in Houston and the Texas Coast. Millions of people were affected; thousands lost their homes, jobs, and livelihoods.

SPECIFIC: Hurricane Irma damaged the US Virgin Islands and neighboring Caribbean nations. Soon after, Hurricane Maria catastrophically devastated Puerto Rico. Months later, Puerto Ricans were still without power and basic necessities. It is still not clear how many have died due to the storm and related damage.

EXAMPLE

In the example below, the paragraph is structured with a topic sentence and specific supporting ideas. This paragraph supports the introduction in the example above.

More people than ever are affected by extreme weather. In 2017, several hurricanes affected the United States and the Caribbean. In Texas, Hurricane Harvey led to historic flooding in Houston and the Texas Coast. Millions of people were affected; thousands lost their homes, jobs, and livelihoods. Hurricane Irma damaged Florida, the US Virgin Islands, and neighboring Caribbean nations. Soon after, Hurricane Maria catastrophically devastated Puerto Rico. Months later, Puerto Ricans were still without power and basic necessities. It is still not clear how many have died due to the storm and related damage. In California, severe droughts led to exceptionally large wildfires that threatened Los Angeles and destroyed neighboring communities. Meanwhile, those same areas—Southern California, the Texas Coast, and Florida—continue to grow, putting more people at risk when the next hurricane or fire strikes.

Writing Well

Using transitions, complex sentences, and certain words can turn a good essay into a great one. Transitions, syntax, word choice, and tone all help clarify and amplify a writer's argument or point and improve the flow of an essay.

TRANSITIONS

An essay consists of several paragraphs. **TRANSITIONS** are words and phrases that help connect the paragraphs and ideas of the text. Most commonly, transitions would appear at the beginning of a paragraph, but writers should also use them throughout a text to connect ideas. Common transitions are words like *also, next, still, although, in addition to,* and *in other words.* A transition shows a relationship between ideas, so writers should pay close attention to the transition words and phrases they choose. Transitions may show connections or contrasts between words and ideas.

Table 3.1. Common Transitions	
TRANSITION TYPE	**EXAMPLES**
addition	additionally, also, as well, further, furthermore, in addition, moreover
cause and effect	as a result, because, consequently, due to, if/then, so, therefore, thus
concluding	briefly, finally, in conclusion, in summary, thus, to conclude
contrast	but, however, in contrast, on the other hand, nevertheless, on the contrary, yet
examples	in other words, for example, for instance
similarity	also, likewise, similarly
time	after, before, currently, later, recently, subsequently, since, then, while

SYNTAX

SYNTAX refers to how words and phrases are arranged in writing or speech. Writing varied sentences is essential to capturing and keeping a reader's interest. A good essay features different types of sentences: simple, complex, compound, and compound-complex. Sentences need not always begin with the subject; they might start with a transition word or phrase, for instance. Variety is key.

Still, writers should keep in mind that the point of an essay is to get an idea across to the reader, so it is most important that writing be clear. They should not sacrifice clarity for the sake of flowery, overly wordy language or confusing syntax.

WORD CHOICE and TONE

Like syntax, word choice makes an impression on readers. The GED does not test on specific vocabulary or require writers to use specific words on the essay. However, the essay is a good opportunity to use strong vocabulary pertaining to the prompt or issue under discussion. Writers should be careful, though, that they understand the words they are using. Writers should also avoid vague, imprecise, or generalizing language like *good*, *bad*, *a lot*, *a little*, *very*, *normal*, and so on.

EDITING, REVISING, and PROOFREADING

On the GED, the writer has a limited amount of time to complete the essay. If there is time for editing or proofreading, writers should hunt for grammar, spelling, or punctuation mistakes that could change the meaning of the text or make it difficult to understand. These include sentence fragments, run-on sentences, subject-verb disagreement, and pronoun-antecedent disagreement.

Test Your Knowledge
TOPIC: DRIVING AGE
IS SIXTEEN TOO YOUNG?

PASSAGE 1: THE CASE FOR TEEN DRIVERS BY RIYA SIDANA

A recent spate of articles appearing in major publications are raising the question of whether states should change the driving age for teens, raising it by one or even two years. The proposals cite statistics about the risks of impulsive, distractible, inexperienced drivers on the road harming themselves and others. Unfortunately, these proposals fail to account for the hardships the change might impose on parents and teens in some families. For instance, some teens provide income by working a part-time job that they might need a car for. Furthermore, the proposals completely overlook other, potentially more useful solutions to the issue.

Teens are indeed inexperienced and impulsive decision makers, and car accidents are the number one cause of death for teens, but raising the driving age will not automatically instill more experience and stronger decision-making. Solutions such as graduated licensing and improved driver's education courses have reduced teen fatalities and road accidents in states that have implemented them, such as New Jersey and Connecticut. These states employ changing requirements for teen drivers that are stricter and harsher for younger drivers and more relaxed as drivers grow more competent. In addition to greater penalties, increasing the amount of supervised driving time and limiting the number of passengers a teen can carry help to gradually improve that teen's skills on the road.

Before eliminating a beloved rite of passage for American teens, inconveniencing families, and demonstrating to teens that that they cannot be trusted, states should seek to address dangers and problems with solutions that have been proven to work.

PASSAGE 2: RAISING THE DRIVING AGE BY THOMAS MADDOW

In 2010, 33 percent of deaths of teens aged sixteen to nineteen were caused by motor vehicle crashes.

Talking on a phone can double the likelihood of an accident, and more than 56 percent of teens admit to using a cell phone while driving.

Of all these groups, sixteen-year-olds have higher crash rates than any other age.

These are just a few of the statistics that demonstrate the need for serious consideration of the age at which we allow our teens to drive. The driving age should be legally raised to seventeen or even eighteen, giving teens time to develop a stronger ability to make responsible choices on the road, avoid the pressures of showing off dangerously for friends, and gain a greater understanding of the responsibilities of a driver. While teens understandably long for the freedom of the road and feel that another year of waiting may be impossible to bear, many other industrialized nations impose an older driving age, and it is the responsibility of adults and lawmakers to do what is best for teens—despite their protests.

PROMPT

The author of passage 1 argues that rather than changing the driving age, states should add limitations and rules for younger drivers. The writer of passage 2 suggests that the correct course is to raise the driving age.

In your response, analyze both texts. Write a persuasive essay explaining which side is more convincing, using examples from each text to support your argument.

TEST YOUR KNOWLEDGE RESPONSE

The argument over whether or not to raise the driving age is not simple, with arguments and statistics supporting both sides. The two passages given both offer compelling reasons why their argument is more correct; however, passage 1 by Riya Sidana offers a more complete argument that addresses a broad audience and includes clear evidence and explanation.

Thomas Maddow's article begins with clear statistics that support his argument, stating them directly and starkly; however, the statistics are missing any context that can help the reader understand how they fit into a larger picture. Sidana, on the other hand, fleshes out her argument that there are better ways to address the issues Maddow lists. She says that "solutions such as graduated licensing and improved driver's education courses have reduced teen fatalities," giving clear examples of how the issues can be addressed without raising the driver's age. By addressing the issues themselves, she makes her argument more complex and complete.

Additionally, Sidana mentions New Jersey and Connecticut to provide specific examples of states that have already done what she suggests. She says these states "employ changing requirements" and that "increasing the amount of supervised driving time and limiting the number of passengers" also helps improve teens' driving skills. In contrast, Maddow calls for action from like-minded adults, citing their responsibilities, but not explaining how the changes will help. Sidana's explanations are more persuasive because they provide more detail.

Finally, Sidana's argument seems to be addressed to a broader audience, both teens who believe they should have the freedom to drive and parents or lawmakers charged with making the changes suggested. Sidana acknowledges the problem rather than dismissing it, but also acknowledges the difficulties that might be faced by families and teens, mentioning that a teen "may provide income." Her language paints teens as potentially responsible, helpful members of the family, but does not deny that they are "inexperienced and impulsive decision makers." By describing both sides impartially, Sidana widens her audience and allows both sides to agree to a compromise.

Because she addresses both sides fairly, makes a more complex argument, and supports it with evidence, Sidana's argument is simply more effective than Maddow's, despite his clear, straightforward statistics. Passage 1 does a better job of persuading its audience.

Follow the link below for your second Reasoning Through Language Arts GED practice test:
http://acceptedinc.com/ged-2018-online-resources

CHAPTER FOUR
Practice Test

Multiple Choice

Read the passage, and then answer the corresponding questions that follow.

Questions 1 – 5 refer to the following passage.

Taking a person's temperature is one of the most basic and common health care tasks. Everyone from nurses to emergency medical technicians to concerned parents should be able to grab a thermometer to take a patient or loved one's temperature. But what's the best way to get an accurate reading? The answer depends on the situation.

The most common way people measure body temperature is orally. A simple digital or disposable thermometer is placed under the tongue for a few minutes, and the task is done. There are many situations, however, when measuring temperature orally isn't an option. For example, when a person can't breathe through his nose, he won't be able to keep his mouth closed long enough to get an accurate reading. In these situations, it's often preferable to place the thermometer in the rectum or armpit. Using the rectum also has the added benefit of providing a much more accurate reading than other locations can provide.

It's also often the case that certain people, like agitated patients or fussy babies, won't be able to sit still long enough for an accurate reading. In these situations, it's best to use a thermometer that works much more quickly, such as one that measures temperature in the ear or at the temporal artery. No matter which method is chosen, however, it's important to check the average temperature for each region, as it can vary by several degrees.

1. Match the site on the body for taking temperature to the phrase that best characterizes it.

	temporal artery	mouth	rectum
most accurate site for taking temperature			
most common site for taking temperature			
best site for taking temperature quickly			

2. Which statement is NOT a detail from the passage?

   A) Taking a temperature in the ear or at the temporal artery is more accurate than taking it orally.

   B) If an individual cannot breathe through the nose, taking his or her temperature orally will likely give an inaccurate reading.

   C) The standard human body temperature varies depending on whether it's measured in the mouth, rectum, armpit, ear, or temporal artery.

   D) The most common way to measure temperature is by placing a thermometer in the mouth.

3. What is the author's primary purpose in writing this essay?

   A) to advocate for the use of thermometers that measure temperature in the ear or at the temporal artery

   B) to explain the methods available to measure a person's temperature and the situation where each method is appropriate

   C) to warn readers that the average temperature of the human body varies by region

   D) to discuss how nurses use different types of thermometers depending on the type of patient they are examining

4. What is the best summary of this passage?

   A) It's important that everyone knows the best way to take a person's temperature in any given situation.

   B) The most common method of taking a person's temperature—orally—isn't appropriate in some situations.

   C) The most accurate way to take a temperature is placing a digital thermometer in the rectum.

   D) There are many different ways to take a person's temperature, and which is appropriate will depend on the situation.

5. According to the passage, why is it sometimes preferable to take a person's temperature rectally?

   A) Rectal readings are more accurate than oral readings.

   B) Many people cannot sit still long enough to have their temperatures taken orally.

   C) Temperature readings can vary widely between regions of the body.

   D) Many people do not have access to quick-acting thermometers.

Questions 6 – 10 refer to the following passage.

In recent decades, jazz has been associated with New Orleans and festivals like Mardi Gras, but in the 1920s, jazz was a booming trend whose influence reached into many aspects of American culture. In fact, the years between World War I and the Great Depression were known as the Jazz Age, a term coined by F. Scott Fitzgerald in his famous novel *The Great Gatsby*. Sometimes also called the Roaring Twenties, this time period saw major urban centers experiencing new economic, cultural, and artistic vitality. In the United States, musicians flocked to cities like New York and Chicago, which would become famous hubs for jazz musicians. Ella Fitzgerald, for example, moved from Virginia to New York City to begin her much-lauded singing career, and jazz pioneer Louis Armstrong got his big break in Chicago.

Jazz music was played by and for a more expressive and freed populace than the United States had previously seen. Women gained the right to vote and were openly seen drinking and dancing to jazz music. This period marked the emergence of the flapper, a woman determined to make a statement about her new role in society. Jazz music also provided the soundtrack for the explosion of African American art and culture now known as the Harlem Renaissance. In addition to Fitzgerald and Armstrong, numerous musicians, including Duke Ellington, Fats Waller, and Bessie Smith, promoted their distinctive and complex music as an integral part of the emerging African American culture.

6. What can the reader conclude from the passage above?

   A) Jazz music was important to minority groups struggling for social equality in the 1920s.

   B) Duke Ellington, Fats Waller, and Bessie Smith were the most important jazz musicians of the Harlem Renaissance.

   C) Women gained the right to vote with the help of jazz musicians.

   D) Duke Ellington, Fats Waller, and Bessie Smith all supported women's right to vote.

7. What can the reader conclude from the passage above?

   A) F. Scott Fitzgerald supported jazz musicians in New York and Chicago.

   B) Jazz music is no longer as popular as it once was.

   C) Both women and African Americans used jazz music as a way of expressing their newfound freedom.

   D) Flappers and African American musicians worked together to produce jazz music.

8. What is the author's primary purpose in writing this essay?

   A) to explain the role jazz musicians played in the Harlem Renaissance

   B) to inform the reader about the many important musicians playing jazz in the 1920s

   C) to discuss how jazz influenced important cultural movements in the 1920s

   D) to provide a history of jazz music in the 20th century

9. Which of the following is NOT a fact stated in the passage?

   A) The years between World War I and the Great Depression were known as the Jazz Age.

   B) Ella Fitzgerald and Louis Armstrong both moved to New York City to start their music careers.

   C) Women danced to jazz music during the 1920s to make a statement about their role in society.

   D) Jazz music was an integral part of the emerging African American culture of the 1920s.

10. Place the name of the public figure in the appropriate column. You may or may not fill up each column.

Ella Fitzgerald	F. Scott Fitzgerald	Duke Ellington	Bessie Smith	Louis Armstrong

Musicians	Writers

Questions 11 – 18 refer to the following passage.

Some (11)_____ lend themselves to controversy and caricatures. In the twenty-first century, police work lands squarely in this category: (12)_____ Still, officers of the law and public investigators play an essential role in our criminal justice system, a role that comes with a great deal of responsibility.

Police officers must possess a number of varied characteristics in order to be successful as representatives of the law. They must first be strong communicators, as they must be able to gather information and effectively communicate that information in written reports. In order to evaluate and respond to situations quickly and appropriately, they must also be highly perceptive and must possess good judgment. In addition, physical strength and stamina are a necessity for officers of the law, as the job can be strenuous and demanding. Finally, they must be empathetic, as they must be able to relate to and treat the people of their community with sincere care and unwavering equity.

To become a police officer, one must complete a rigorous series of hiring requirements, (13)_____ with providing proof of citizenship, age, education, and criminal history. After meeting these basic requirements, each candidate must pass a series of (14)_____ to determine (15)_____ First, the candidate must pass a series of challenging physical tests and written exams, which are intended to evaluate the candidate based on his or her physical and mental fitness. Then, each candidate must pass a series of challenging interviews, during which he or she may be asked to complete lie detector and drug tests. Finally, an applicant who meets all of these requirements must gain acceptance into (16)_____ academy to begin training.

Academy training is extensive for officers of the law. In addition to physical training in (17)_____ candidates must also complete a series of classes in constitutional law, state and local law, civil rights, and ethics. Federal agents or officers with specialized responsibilities must complete even more training.

An officer who is successful in his or her initial role as patrolman or first responder may find him- or herself in the position of receiving a promotion. Often, this first promotion elevates the person to the role of detective or special investigator. Detectives and special investigators are responsible for (18)_____ in specialized areas such as homicide, vice, or special victims.

11.

    A) careers, especially those in the public eye,

    B) careers—especially those in the public eye

    C) careers, especially those in the public eye—

    D) careers, especially those in the public eye

12.

    A) crooked cops and detectives with donuts are commonplace in the worlds of media and entertainment.

    B) however, it is an extremely challenging profession, and its significance should not be underestimated.

    C) the work itself is challenging, but the perks that come along with it are substantial.

    D) most people admire and respect officers of the law.

17.

A) self-defense firearms, emergency response and first aid,

B) self-defense, firearms, emergency response, and first aid,

C) self-defense, firearms, emergency, response and first aid,

D) self-defense, firearms emergency, response, and first aid,

18.

A) investigating reported crimes, to gather and protecting evidence, conducting interviews, and for solving crimes

B) investigate reported crimes, gather and protecting evidence, conduct interviews, and solve crimes

C) investigating reported crimes, gathering and protecting evidence, conducting interviews, and solving crimes

D) investigation reported crimes, to gather and protect evidence, to conduct interview, and solving crimes

13.

A) which begin

B) which begins

C) that begin

D) that begins

14.

A) evaluations, which are intended

B) evaluations, they are intended

C) evaluations, being intended

D) evaluations—these are intended

15.

A) our suitability for police work.

B) its suitability for police work.

C) his or her suitability for police work.

D) the suitability for police work.

16.

A) his or her agency's

B) his or her agencies

C) their agencies

D) their agency's

Questions 19–24 refer to the following passage.

The most important part of brewing coffee is getting the right water. Choose a water that you think has a nice, neutral flavor. Anything with too many minerals or contaminants will change the flavor of the coffee, and water with too few minerals won't do a good job of extracting the flavor from the coffee beans. Water should be heated to between 195 and 205 degrees Fahrenheit. Boiling water (212 degrees Fahrenheit) will burn the beans and give your coffee a scorched flavor.

While the water is heating, grind your beans. Remember, the fresher the grind, the fresher the flavor of the coffee. The number of beans is entirely dependent on your personal taste. Obviously, more beans will result in a more robust flavor, while fewer beans will give your coffee a more subtle taste. The texture of the grind should be not too fine (which can lead to bitter coffee) or too large (which can lead to weak coffee).

Once the beans are ground and the water has reached the perfect temperature, you're ready to brew. A French press (which we recommend), allows you to control brewing time and provide a thorough brew. Pour the grounds into the press, then pour the hot water over the grounds and let it steep. The brew shouldn't require more than five minutes, although those of you who like your coffee a bit harsher can leave it longer. Finally, use the plunger to remove the grounds and pour.

19. Which of the following statements based on the passage should be considered an opinion?

   A) While the water is heating, grind your beans.

   B) A French press (which we recommend), allows you to control brewing time and provide a thorough brew.

   C) Anything with too many minerals or contaminants will change the flavor of the coffee, and water with too few minerals won't do a good job of extracting the flavor from the coffee beans.

   D) Finally, use the plunger to remove the grounds and pour.

20. Which of the following conclusions is best supported by the passage?

   A) Coffee should never be brewed for longer than five minutes.

   B) It's better to use too many coffee beans when making coffee than too few.

   C) Brewing quality coffee at home is too complicated for most people to do well.

   D) The best way to brew coffee is often determined by personal preferences.

21. What is the author's intent in writing this passage?

   A) to describe how to make hot beverages

   B) to argue that grinding beans makes a better cup of coffee

   C) to claim that coffee is better than tea

   D) to explain how to brew a cup of coffee

22. Which of the following best describes the structure of the text?

   A) chronological

   B) cause and effect

   C) problem and solution

   D) contrast

23. Which of the following would be an appropriate title for this passage?

   A) How to Brew the Perfect Cup of Coffee

   B) Why Drinking Coffee Is the Best Way to Start the Day

   C) How to Use a French Press to Make Coffee

   D) The Importance of Grinding Coffee Beans

24. Arrange the following boxes in order from first to last in the order they appear in the passage.

Grind the beans and put them in the French press.	Choose the right type of water.	Pour the hot water over the grounds and let the coffee steep.	Heat it to the correct tempera-ture.
First			
Second			
Third			
Fourth			

Questions 25 – 29 refer to the following passage.

Bioluminescence, the ability to create light, is an adaptation that is most present in animals that live in primarily dark environments like the ocean. It is caused by a chemical reaction in the animal's body, which allows the animal to fulfill a particular need. Like other types of adaptations, bioluminescence serves a different function in each species that displays the ability; however, for the most part, these functions can be divided into three categories: (25)_____

For many ocean-dwelling, bioluminescent creatures, the ability to create light serves a defensive function. The vampire squid, for example, uses the light to stun and confuse its predators. Unlike other squid, which may emit a dark liquid to confuse predators, the vampire squid has adapted to a deep ocean environment—where light is limited and dark liquid has no effect. As a result, the vampire squid instead emits (26)_____ which (27)_____ while the squid escapes capture.

Bioluminescence serves other defensive purposes as well. Some species, like the hatchet fish, use their own light to create a sort of camouflage: (28)_____ Mis-direction is also a common application of bioluminescence. Some animals, like the brittle star, can detach lit body parts and leave (29)_____

With its commonality among species and its variety of applications, bioluminescence is a fascinating topic that can enliven our senses and spark our curiosities about the natural world.

25.

A) protection, hunting, and reproduction.

B) for protection, to hunt, and reproduction.

C) protecting, to hunt, and reproducing.

D) in protection, hunting, and to reproduce.

27.

A) surprises their predators and distracts them

B) surprises its predators and distracts it

C) surprise their predators and distracts them

D) surprises its predator and distracts it

28.

A) when a predator is swimming, below, a lit underbelly allows the prey to swim along unnoticed blending in with the light from above.

B) when a predator is swimming below, a lit underbelly allows the prey to swim along unnoticed, blending in with the light from above.

C) when a predator is swimming below a lit underbelly allows the prey to swim along unnoticed, blending in, with the light from above.

D) when a predator is swimming below, a lit underbelly, allows the prey to swim along unnoticed, blending in, with the light from above.

26. Which of the following is most appropriate considering the tone and purpose of the passage?

A) a bright, nasty gunk,

B) a secretion of organic, bioluminescent matter,

C) the brightest, weirdest goop you ever saw,

D) a glowing goo,

29.

A) them behind in order to draw predators away from themselves.

B) it behind in order to draw predators away from itself.

C) them behind in order to draw predators away from itself.

D) it behind in order to draw predators away from themselves.

Questions 30–35 refer to the following passage.

Influenza (also called the flu) has historically been one of the most common, and deadliest, human infections. While many people who contract the virus will recover, many others will not. Over the past 150 years, tens of millions of people have died from the flu, and millions more have been left with lingering complications such as secondary infections.

Although it's a common disease, the flu is not actually highly infectious, meaning it's relatively difficult to contract. The flu can only be transmitted when individuals come into direct contact with bodily fluids of people infected with the flu or when they are exposed to expelled aerosol particles (which result from coughing and sneezing). Because the viruses can only travel short distances as aerosol particles and will die within a few hours on hard surfaces, the virus can be contained with fairly simple health measures like hand washing and face masks.

However, the spread of the flu can only be contained when people are aware such measures need to be taken. One of the reasons the flu has historically been so deadly is the amount of time between when people become infectious and when they develop symptoms. Viral shedding—the process by which the body releases viruses that have been successfully reproducing during the infection—takes place two days after infection, while symptoms do not usually develop until the third day of infection. Thus, infected individuals have at least twenty-four hours in which they may unknowingly infect others.

30. What is the main idea of the passage?
    A) The flu is a deadly disease that's difficult to control because people become infectious before they show symptoms.
    B) For the flu to be transmitted, individuals must come in contact with bodily fluids from infected individuals.
    C) The spread of the flu is easy to contain because the viruses do not live long either as aerosol particles or on hard surfaces.
    D) The flu has killed tens of millions of people and can often cause deadly secondary infections.

32. Why is the flu considered to not be highly infectious?
    A) Many people who get the flu will recover and have no lasting complications, so only a small number of people who become infected will die.
    B) The process of viral shedding takes two days, so infected individuals have enough time to implement simple health measures that stop the spread of the disease.
    C) The flu virus cannot travel far or live for long periods of time outside the human body, so its spread can easily be contained.
    D) Twenty-four hours is a relatively short period of time for the virus to spread among a population.

31. Which of the following correctly describes the flu?
    A) The flu is easy to contract and always fatal.
    B) The flu is difficult to contract and always fatal.
    C) The flu is easy to contract and sometimes fatal.
    D) The flu is difficult to contract and sometimes fatal.

33. What is the meaning of the word *measures* in the second paragraph?
    A) a plan of action
    B) a standard unit
    C) an adequate amount
    D) a rhythmic movement

34. Which statement is NOT a detail from the passage?
    A) Tens of millions of people have been killed by the flu virus.
    B) There is typically a twenty-four hour window during which individuals are infectious but not showing flu symptoms.
    C) Viral shedding is the process by which people recover from the flu.
    D) The flu can be transmitted by direct contact with bodily fluids from infected individuals or by exposure to aerosol particles.

35. What can the reader conclude from the previous passage?

A) Preemptively implementing health measures like hand washing and face masks could help stop the spread of the flu virus.

B) Doctors are not sure how the flu virus is transmitted, so they are unsure how to stop it from spreading.

C) The flu is dangerous because it is both deadly and highly infectious.

D) Individuals stop being infectious three days after they are infected.

Questions 36 – 42 refer to the following passage.

Dr. Martin Kemp sat at his computer sifting through emails. (36)_____ Then he came across an email from someone named Peter. The subject read: *Leonardo?*

Another loony, Kemp thought. (37)_____ He received these emails fairly regularly, two or three times a week most weeks, and he had yet to come across an inquiry that even gave him pause. As Professor Emeritus of Art History at Oxford University, Kemp was a da Vinci expert, and he regularly received notes from people thinking they had come across a lost work of the great artist. He had no reason to believe this one was any different.

Then he opened the image.

A feeling of utter astonishment fell over Kemp. He put down his coffee, stopped shuffling papers, and stared at the high-resolution image on his screen. He moved his chair (38)_____ to get a better look at the striking portrait. He looked at it in its full form for a number of minutes before zooming in to get a better view. The detail work was magnificent, and the portrait seemed to have a life about it. (39)_____ Kemp thought. He decided to respond to the inquiry: he would travel to Zurich, at no fee to the owner of the piece, to (40)_____ the work in person.

Outside of his vault in Zurich, Peter Silverman slowly pulled the mysterious portrait out of its protective envelope. He could not believe he was finally here. When he first lost the auction of the portrait almost a decade before, he thought he would never see it again. Now, he held it in his gloved hands, discussing its potential origins with one of the world's leading experts. He laid the portrait down carefully in front of Martin Kemp and waited for the (41)_____.

Kemp stared silently down at the piece. A rush of energy rolled over him, a feeling he would later have trouble describing in words. He only knew that this portrait was special, unlike any of the works he had evaluated before. (42)_____ Her eyes had been drawn to show her vitality, and her hair seemed to respond naturally to the pressure of the headdress that hugged her head. *These details...* Kemp thought to himself, trailing off. He could not know by that time, of course, whether the portrait was actually the work of the great da Vinci, but he knew he wanted to investigate further.

36. What sentence would be most effective if inserted here?

A) Some he responded to quickly, while marking others for later, still others he deleted immediately.

B) Some he responded to quickly, others he marked for later, and still others he deleted immediately.

C) Some he would respond to quickly, and others he marked for later, still others he would delete.

D) Some he is responding to quickly, others he would mark for later, still others he deletes immediately.

37.

A) He scoffed a little but clicking to open the message anyway.

B) He scoffed a little and clicking to open the message anyway.

C) He scoffed a little but clicked to open the message anyway.

D) He scoffs a little but clicking to open the message anyway.

38.

A) closer to his desk, and attempting

B) closer to his desk, attempting

C) closer to his desk as though

D) closer to his desk; next he was attempting

39. Which choice best expresses Dr. Kemp's cautious interest in the image?

A) *Uncanny,*

B) *That's weird,*

C) *It must be a da Vinci,*

D) *Stellar,*

40.

A) eyeball

B) inspect

C) display

D) contemplate

41.

A) connoisseur's expert opinion

B) connoisseur's opinion

C) educated connoisseur's opinion

D) educated connoisseur's expert opinion

42.

A) The subject of the portrait, a young woman, appeared composed and thoughtful, as one who was living in a world that required her to act, by today's standards, well beyond her age.

B) A young woman, the subject of the portrait, appearing composed and thoughtful, as one living in a world, by today's standards, that required her to act well beyond her age.

C) The subject of the portrait, a young woman who was living, by today's standards, in a world that required her to act well beyond her age, appeared composed and thoughtful.

D) Composed and thoughtful, a young woman, the subject of the portrait, appearing composed and thoughtful, was living in a world that required her to act well beyond her age by today's standards.

Questions 43–47 refer to the following passage.

It had been a long morning for Julia. She'd been woken up early by the sound of lawn mowers outside her window, and despite her best efforts, had been unable to get back to sleep. So, she'd reluctantly got out of bed, showered, and prepared her morning cup of coffee. At least, she tried to anyway. In the kitchen she'd discovered she was out of regular coffee and had to settle for a decaffeinated cup instead.

Once on the road, her caffeine-free mug of coffee didn't help make traffic less annoying. In fact, it seemed to Julia like the other drivers were sluggish and surly as well—it took her an extra fifteen minutes to get to work. And when she arrived, all the parking spots were full.

By the time she'd finally found a spot in the overflow lot, she was thirty minutes late for work. She'd hoped her boss would be too busy to notice, but he'd already put a pile of paperwork on her desk with a note that simply said "Rewrite." She wondered if she should point out to her boss that she hadn't been the one to write the reports in the first place, but decided against it.

When the fire alarm went off an hour later, Julia decided she'd had enough. She grabbed her purse and headed outside with her coworkers. While everyone else stood around waiting for the alarm to quiet, Julia determinedly walked to her car, fired up the engine, and set a course for home.

43. Which of the following lists Julia's actions in the correct sequence?
- **A)** Julia woke up early and found she didn't have any regular coffee. When she got to work, her boss had a lot for her to do. When the fire alarm went off, she decided to go home.
- **B)** Julia got to work and decided she was too tired to do the work her boss asked for, so she went home to get a cup of coffee.
- **C)** Julia woke up when the fire alarm went off and couldn't get back to sleep. She then got stuck in traffic and arrived at work thirty minutes late.
- **D)** Julia was woken up early by a lawnmower and then got stuck in traffic on the way to her office. Once there, she found that the office was out of coffee and she had a lot of work to do. When the fire alarm went off, she decided to go home.

44. Which of the following is the most likely reason Julia did not return to work after the alarm?
- **A)** She was embarrassed that she could not finish the work her boss asked for.
- **B)** She was tired and wanted to go home.
- **C)** She got stuck in traffic and could not get back to her office.
- **D)** Her boss gave her the afternoon off.

45. Which of the following statements based on the passage should be considered an opinion?

A) Julia's boss asked her to do work to help one of her coworkers.

B) Julia was late to work because of traffic.

C) It was irresponsible for Julia to leave work early.

D) Julia was tired because she'd been woken up early.

46. The passage states that Julia set a course for home. Which of the following is the most accurate interpretation of this sentence?

A) Julia is looking up directions to her house.

B) Julia is planning to drive home.

C) Julia wants to go home but will go back to work.

D) Julia is worried the fire at her office will spread to her home.

47. Which of the following conclusions is best supported by the passage?

A) Julia will find a job closer to her home.

B) Julia will be fired.

C) Julia will feel guilty and return to work.

D) Julia will drive home and go to sleep.

Questions 48–55 refer to the following passage.

Across the United States, a new trend in dining has taken (48)_____ like Austin, Portland, San Francisco, and Seattle are seeing a significant increase in one particular type of dining establishment—the food truck. Though the modern food truck phenomenon is still in (49)_____ prime, mobile dining is in no way (50)_____: precursors to the modern food truck can be traced back as far as the 1800s.

The earliest predecessors to the modern food truck (51)_____; in fact, they were not motorized at all. Push carts were some of the earliest vehicles for mobile food distribution and were popular in urban areas like New York City, where workers needed access to quick, cheap lunches. (52)_____ while these carts were mobile, they were not equipped with the tools necessary to prepare the food.

In the late 1800s, two new inventions marked important milestones in the development of the modern food truck. In 1866, Charles Goodnight created the first (53)_____ that served as a mobile kitchen for cowmen who were herding cattle northward for sale. The cooks, or "cookies," who traveled with the cowmen would wake early and prepare meals of beans, dried meats, and biscuits using the tools and ingredients on the chuck wagon. Similarly, in 1872, a food vendor named Walter Scott conceived of the lunch wagon, from which he would serve sandwiches, coffee, and desserts to journalists outside a Providence, Rhode Island, newspaper office.

In the 1900s, mobile dining took even newer forms, as the invention of motorized transportation began to transform the industry. During the World War II era, mobile canteens popped up near army bases to serve quick, easy meals to the troops. Ice cream trucks followed in the 1950s, serving children and adults alike cold treats on hot summer afternoons. In the 1960s, large food service trucks called "roach coaches" began to pop up near densely populated urban areas, often serving cheap meals from grungy kitchens.

(54)_____ the food truck industry has transformed the mobile dining experience from one of convenience to one of excitement. Today, city dwellers and tourists (55)_____ to food trucks not only for ease and affordability, but also for unique foods, new flavors, and fun experiences. In some places, whole streets or even neighborhoods are devoted to hosting these food trucks, and people travel from all over the city to try what they're offering.

48.
   A) hold. Cities
   B) hold in cities
   C) hold of cities
   D) hold, cities

49.
   A) it's
   B) its
   C) its'
   D) it is

50.
   A) a unique, novel idea
   B) a new or novel idea
   C) a novel idea
   D) a uniquely novel idea

51.
   A) was actually not a truck
   B) were actually not trucks
   C) are actually not trucks
   D) is actually not a truck

52.
   A) Instead,
   B) However,
   C) As a result,
   D) Therefore,

53.
   A) chuck wagon and a covered wagon
   B) chuck wagon, and a covered wagon
   C) chuck wagon, a covered wagon
   D) chuck wagon; a covered wagon

54.
   A) In recent years,
   B) Consequently,
   C) Therefore,
   D) In conclusion,

55.
   A) will have flocked
   B) are flocking
   C) have flocked
   D) have been flocking

The Essay

TECHNOLOGY in the CLASSROOM: HELPFUL or a DISTRACTION?

Passage 1: iGen: Distracted Learning in the Age of the Internet by Sarah Gilliam

Walk into a classroom in a modern 1:1 school (schools that provide computers to all students), and you might be surprised. Instead of rows of desks filled with students facing the front, paper and pencil at the ready, there are rows of computer screens and students typing diligently. However, what looks like a productive, innovative class environment can be deceiving.

Schools and students are embracing technology in service of learning, but at what cost? Studies demonstrate again and again that students who use computers to take notes are distracted and retain less information than those who handwrite their notes. Many students admit to being distracted by their phones and computers, surfing the internet or checking email rather than tuning in to the teacher or class. Students can even be distracted when their peers are surfing the internet.

While some technology is undeniably useful in the classroom—presentation technology like projectors and PowerPoint, for instance—other applications are more distraction than boon. Student technology use should be carefully monitored by instructors and used only in situations where the technology creates beneficial opportunities—for instance, email and group chats to enhance after-school group work or tutorials. Technology is here to stay—it would be foolish to deny that. However, it should be used wisely, not widely.

Passage 2: High Tech Classrooms Are the Future of Education by Diedrich Elton

Imagine you are a student in a modern high school: At the beginning of your day, you check your phone to remember what assignments are due today; you text a friend with a question about the algebra homework; and then you head to school, where you cycle through classes that include using the internet to research local water-use rates versus national, plot points on a graph, create a group presentation using sharing programs, and record all your notes and homework in a digital file. You email teachers and chat with friends, and your phone helps you get text reminders about homework from teachers.

All these actions are possible due to the advent of 1:1 technology in many classrooms, which allows students and teachers to stay connected to the wider world and do many new and exciting things that were not possible before computers became broadly used and available. Putting technology in the classroom gives opportunities to all students, even those who might not be able to afford that technology at home. It provides the chance to learn vital skills for a future job.

Schools should embrace technology in the classroom and use every opportunity to inject new learning technology into student work: Student creativity will shine and students will be well prepared for their futures.

Prompt

The author of passage 1 argues that technology is distracting and should be monitored and limited by instructors. The writer of passage 2 encourages complete adoption and embracing of technological advancements in the classroom.

In your response, analyze both texts. Write a persuasive essay explaining which side is more convincing, using examples from each text to support your argument.

Answer Key
MULTIPLE CHOICE

1.

most accurate site for taking temperature	rectum
most common site for taking temperature	mouth
best site for taking temperature quickly	temporal artery

2. A) is correct. This detail is not stated in the passage.

3. B) is correct. In the first paragraph, the author writes, "But what's the best way to get an accurate reading? The answer depends on the situation." She then goes on to describe various options and their applications.

4. B) is correct. The author indicates that "[t]he most common way people measure body temperature is orally" but that "[t]here are many situations [...] when measuring temperature orally isn't an option." She then goes on to describe these situations in the second and third paragraphs.

5. A) is correct. The second paragraph of the passage states that "[u]sing the rectum also has the added benefit of providing a much more accurate reading than other locations can provide."

6. A) is correct. The author writes that "[j]azz music was played by and for a more expressive and freed populace than the United States had previously seen." In addition to "the emergence of the flapper[,]" the 1920s saw "the explosion of African American art and culture now known as the Harlem Renaissance."

7. C) is correct. The author writes that "[j]azz music was played by and for a more expressive and freed populace than the United States had previously seen." In addition to "the emergence of the flapper[,]" the 1920s saw "the explosion of African American art and culture now known as the Harlem Renaissance."

8. C) is correct. The author opens the passage saying, "In recent decades, jazz has been associated with New Orleans and festivals like Mardi Gras, but in the 1920s, jazz was a booming trend whose influence reached into many aspects of American culture." He then goes on to elaborate on what these movements were.

9. B) is correct. At the end of the first paragraph, the author writes, "Ella Fitzgerald, for example, moved from Virginia to New York City to begin her much-lauded singing career, and jazz pioneer Louis Armstrong got his big break in Chicago."

10.

Musicians	Writers
Ella Fitzgerald	
Duke Ellington	F. Scott Fitzgerald
Bessie Smith	
Louis Armstrong	

11. A) is correct. The two commas correctly set off the adjectival phrase *especially those in the* *public eye*, which describes the noun *careers*.

12. **A) is correct.** Earlier in the paragraph, the author says that careers such as law enforcement "lend themselves to controversy and caricatures." The phrase *crooked cops and detectives with donuts* supports these claims.

13. **B) is correct.** The singular noun *series* agrees with the singular verb *begins*. Also, the relative pronoun *which* is correctly used here: the opening phrase *To become... requirements* can stand on its own as a sentence. This means that the phrase beginning with *which* is not needed to complete the thought.

14. **A) is correct.** The relative pronoun *which* is correctly used here: the opening phrase *After meeting... evaluations* can stand on its own as a sentence. Also, the plural noun *evaluations* agrees with the plural verb *are*.

15. **C) is correct.** The possessive pronouns *his* and *her* agree with the antecedent *each candidate*, which is singular.

16. **A) is correct.** The possessive pronouns *his* and *her* agree with the antecedent *an applicant*, which is singular. Also, *agency's* correctly uses an apostrophe and *s* to show possession.

17. **B) is correct.** All four commas appear in the correct places, including the serial comma that precedes the word *and*.

18. **C) is correct.** All verbs in the series parallel one another grammatically: *investigating*,

gathering, protecting, conducting, and *solving*.

19. **B) is correct.** The writer uses the first person, showing his or her opinion, to recommend a French press as the best way to brew coffee.

20. **D) is correct.** The passage mentions several times that decisions about things like water minerals, ground size, and steep time will depend on the preference of the coffee drinker.

21. **D) is correct.** This passage is a step-by-step explanation of how to brew a cup of coffee.

22. **A) is correct.** The author describes the steps for making coffee in chronological order.

23. **A) is correct.** The passage as a whole describes from start to finish how to make a cup of coffee the drinker will enjoy.

24.

First	Choose the right type of water.
Second	Heat it to the correct temperature.
Third	Grind the beans and put them in the French press.
Fourth	Pour the hot water over the grounds and let the coffee steep.

25. **A) is correct.** The series of three nouns, *protection, hunting, and reproduction*, is correctly punctuated. Parallel construction allows the phrase to read smoothly.

26. **D) is correct.** This phrase is appropriate to the passage's tone and purpose. It is short, yet it provides a vivid, accurate description of the substance that the squid emits.

27. **D) is correct.** The singular verb *surprises* agrees with the singular noun *goo*. Also, the singular possessive pronoun *its* agrees with the singular noun phrase *the vampire squid*. Finally, the singular noun *predator* agrees with the singular object pronoun *it* in *distracts it*.

28. **B) is correct.** Both commas are correctly placed.

29. **A) is correct.** The plural pronoun *them* agrees with the plural noun *parts*. Also, the plural reflexive pronoun *themselves* agrees with the plural noun *animals*.

30. **A) is correct.** This choice addresses all of the main ideas of the passage: the flu is potentially deadly, highly infectious, and difficult to contain due to viral shedding.

31. **D) is correct.** According to the passage, "the flu is...relatively difficult to contract," and "[w]hile many people who contract the virus will recover, many others will not."

32. **C) is correct.** The second paragraph states that the flu is "relatively difficult to contract" because it "can only be transmitted when individuals come into direct contact with bodily fluids of people infected with the flu or when they are exposed to expelled aerosol particles[.]"

33. **A) is correct.** The author uses the term *measures* to describe the steps that people take to prevent the spreading of the influenza virus.

34. **C) is correct.** The final paragraph of the passage states that viral shedding is "the process by which the body releases viruses that have been successfully reproducing during the infection."

35. **A) is correct.** The second paragraph of the passage states that "the virus can be contained with fairly simple health measures like hand washing and face masks."

36. **B) is correct.** This sentence's three past-tense verbs agree with one another. The author uses parallel structure effectively.

37. **C) is correct.** The two past-tense verbs, *scoffed* and *clicked*, agree.

38. **B) is correct.** This sentence is succinct and grammatical. It describes Kemp's action and tells why he does what he does.

39. **A) is correct.** The adjective *uncanny* shows that Kemp is awed by the mysterious image.

40. **B) is correct.** The verb *inspect* shows exactly what Kemp plans to do when he sees the artwork in person.

41. **B) is correct.** "Connoisseur's expert opinion" is redundant, so it is correct to delete either *connoisseur* or *expert*.

42. **A) is correct.** This sentence is well constructed and correctly punctuated. It reads smoothly and its meaning is clear.

43. **A) is correct.** This choice describes the order of Julia's actions that matches chronological order of the passage.

44. **B) is correct.** The passage describes how Julia had an exhausting morning, and it can be assumed that when "she'd had enough" she decided to go home.

45. **C) is correct.** Whether it was irresponsible for Julia to leave work is a matter of opinion. Some readers may agree, and others may disagree. The other statements are facts that can be proven from the passage.

46. **B) is correct.** The phrase "set a course for home" is an idiom that means to head in a certain direction, so Julia is planning to go home.

47. **D) is correct.** The passage emphasizes that Julia is tired, so she's most likely going to drive home and go to sleep.

48. **A) is correct.** Since the second sentence is already so long, it is probably best not to combine the two.

49. **B) is correct.** The singular neuter possessive pronoun *its* agrees with its singular neuter antecedent, *phenomenon*.

50. **C) is correct.** Using just one adjective, *novel*, saves the phrase from being redundant.

51. **B) is correct.** The plural verb *were* agrees with the plural noun *predecessors*.

52. **B) is correct.** The adverb *however* makes good sense here. It paves the way for the author to say something negative about push carts that contrasts with their positive qualities.

53. **C) is correct.** This construction correctly conveys the idea that a chuck wagon was a covered wagon that served as a kitchen.

54. **A) is correct.** The adverbial phrase *in recent years* makes good sense here. It fits in with the phrase *a new trend*, which appears earlier in the passage.

55. **B) is correct.** The progressive verb tense in *are flocking* makes good sense here. The author is describing events that are happening in the present day.

Sample Essay

While both passages describe some benefits of using technology in education, passage 1 cautions that there are possible drawbacks, while passage 2 encourages schools to fully embrace all aspects of educational technology. Sarah Gilliam's argument in passage 1 is more convincing because it uses a reasonable, moderate tone that encourages compromise and provides specific examples of the drawbacks of technology.

Gilliam begins her argument with a description of modern schools that shows students who are "diligently...taking notes." She says, "Schools and students are embracing technology in service of learning." Her descriptions are positive and she concedes that schools and students have good intentions with the use of text, making her tone seem reasonable. The moderate tone helps the audience trust Gilliam's argument more than Diedrich Elton's, whose positive descriptions are enthusiastic and leave no room for doubt. Elton describes technology use as an "opportunity" that will allow "creativity to shine." Comparatively, Gilliam is more effective because she is more moderate.

Gilliam uses a moderate tone because she wants the audience to approach technology use through compromise, rather than either embracing it fully or rejecting it fully. She says that "it would be foolish to deny" that schools will continue to use tech and admits that it has been valuable, but that schools should use it in situations that create "new, beneficial opportunities" rather than for everything. She calls on technology use to be "carefully monitored" and used "wisely, not widely." Gilliam argues for a compromise that allows both sides to agree, unlike Elton, who does not mention any downsides to technology or permit a compromise.

Finally, Gilliam also supports her argument by mentioning studies that show that students who take notes on computers are "distracted and retain less information," providing a reason for her caution. By supporting her own points while acknowledging the opposing side, Gilliam provides a reason to trust her encouragement to compromise. She lists several ways technology can be a distraction, and these distractions contrast with the effective uses she lists later—"group chats to enhance...group work or tutorials" and "presentation technology like projectors and PowerPoint."

Passage 1 by Gilliam more effectively presents an argument through a moderate tone, compromise, and strong support, in contrast to the enthusiasm and imagination of passage 2.

Made in the USA
Middletown, DE
12 July 2021